WHAT IS THE BOOK OF PSALMS?

Kids' Guides to God's Word Series

What Is the Book of Genesis?
What Is the Book of Exodus?
What Is the Book of Leviticus?
What Is the Book of Numbers?
What Is the Book of Deuteronomy?
What Is the Book of Joshua?
What Is the Book of Judges?
What Is the Book of Ruth?
What Is the Book of 1 Samuel?
What Is the Book of 2 Samuel?
What Is the Book of 1 Kings?
What Is the Book of 2 Kings?
What Are the Books of 1–2 Chronicles?
What Are the Books of Ezra & Nehemiah?
What Is the Book of Esther?
What Is the Book of Job?
What Is the Book of Psalms?
What Is the Book of Proverbs?
What Is the Book of Ecclesiastes?
What Are the Books of Song of Songs &
Lamentations?
What Is the Book of Isaiah?
What Is the Book of Jeremiah?
What Is the Book of Ezekiel?
What Is the Book of Daniel?
What Are the Books of Hosea–Micah?
What Are the Books of Nahum–Malachi?

What Is the Gospel of Matthew?
What Is the Gospel of Mark?
What Is the Gospel of Luke?
What Is the Gospel of John?
What Is the Book of Acts?
What Is the Book of Romans?
What Is the Book of 1 Corinthians?
What Is the Book of 2 Corinthians?
What Is the Book of Galatians?
What Is the Book of Ephesians?
What Is the Book of Philippians?
What Are the Books of Colossians
& Philemon?
What Are the Books of 1–2 Thessalonians?
What Are the Books of 1–2 Timothy & Titus?
What Is the Book of Hebrews?
What Is the Book of James?
What Are the Books of 1–2 Peter & Jude?
What Are the Books of 1–3 John?
What Is the Book of Revelation?

What Is the Book of

PSALMS?

Michael Whitworth

ISBN 978-1-971767-25-3

Published by Start2Finish
Bend, Oregon 97702
start2finish.org

Printed in the United States of America
30 29 28 27 26   1 2 3 4 5

CONTENTS

INTRODUCTION

Have you ever noticed that music finds you before you find it? You don't usually sit down and think, "I need a song right now." It just happens. You're in the car and a song comes on that matches exactly how you feel. You're lying in bed at night and a melody gets stuck in your head that says something you couldn't say yourself. You hear a song at a friend's house, or at church, or in a movie, and something inside you goes, *Yes. That's it. That's the thing I didn't know how to put into words.*

Music does something that regular talking can't. It gets underneath your defenses. A conversation about sadness is one thing. A sad song is something else entirely. A lecture about courage might inspire you for an afternoon. A song about courage can carry you through a year. There's a reason people don't just read their wedding vows at weddings. They play songs. There's a reason soldiers don't just march in silence. They sing.

Now imagine a book in the Bible that works like that. Not a history book. Not a law book. Not a letter or a prophecy. A songbook. One hundred and fifty songs, written over the course of a thousand years, covering every single thing a human being can feel, and designed to be sung out loud by real people in real pain and real joy and real confusion.

That's the book of Psalms. And it might be the most important book in the Bible you've never really studied.

MORE THAN YOU THINK

Everybody knows pieces of the Psalms. "The LORD is my shepherd, I shall not want." "Be still, and know that I am God." "This is the day the LORD has made; let us rejoice and be glad in it." These lines show up on posters, in greeting cards, at funerals and weddings and graduations. They're some of the most quoted words in human history.

But here's what most people miss: those familiar verses are just the surface. Underneath them is a book that is far more raw, more honest, more complicated, and more powerful than most people realize.

The Psalms don't just praise God. They yell at him. They accuse him of forgetting. They ask "How long?" and "Why?" and "Where are you?" They describe enemies in language that would make your skin crawl. They confess sins so devastating that the writer begs God to create something entirely new inside him. They wrestle with the brutal unfairness of watching wicked people prosper while the faithful suffer. They ask God to break teeth, pour out wrath, and destroy the people who have done unspeakable things.

And then, sometimes in the very same poem, they turn around and say, "But I trust you."

The Psalms are not safe. They are not tidy. They are not the gentle, soothing background music that most people think they are. They are the most emotionally honest collection of writing in the entire Bible, and once you actually read them, they will change the way you talk to God.

THE SOUNDTRACK TO THE WHOLE STORY

Unlike most books of the Bible, the Psalms don't pick up where another book left off. There's no "story so far" because the Psalms aren't a story. They're a collection, written by dozens of different people across nearly a thousand years of Israel's history.

But the Psalms sit at the center of a story you already know.

You know about creation, when God made a world and called it good. The Psalms celebrate that: "The heavens declare the glory of God; the skies proclaim the work of his hands" (Psalm 19:1).

You know about the exodus, when God rescued his people from slavery in Egypt. The Psalms retell that story again and again, reminding Israel never to forget what God did for them.

You know about the wilderness, where the people grumbled and complained and tested God's patience for forty years. The Psalms remember that too, as a warning to the next generation not to make the same mistakes.

You know about David, the shepherd boy who became king. David wrote nearly half the psalms in the book, and his voice echoes through every corner of it, from the highest praise to the lowest grief.

You know about the exile, when Babylon destroyed Jerusalem, leveled the temple, and dragged God's people away from everything they loved. The Psalms contain some of the most anguished songs ever written about that loss: "By the rivers of Babylon we sat and wept when we remembered Zion" (Psalm 137:1).

And you know about Jesus. He grew up singing these songs. He quoted them in his teaching. He prayed them in the garden. He cried one of them from the cross. The New Testament quotes the Psalms more than almost any other Old Testament book, because the early Christians recognized that these ancient songs had been pointing to Jesus all along.

The Psalms aren't one chapter of Israel's story. They're the soundtrack to the whole thing.

WHAT YOU'RE ABOUT TO READ

Here's what you're going to find in this book. We'll start by learning what the Psalms actually are: who wrote them, how they're organized, and why they ended up at the center of the Bible. Then we'll learn how to read them, because poetry doesn't work the same way stories do, and if you read a psalm like you read a chapter of 1 Samuel, you'll miss most of what's happening.

After that, we'll walk through every major type of psalm in the book. You'll discover that the Psalms aren't random. They fall into categories, and each category captures a different experience of life with God.

There are psalms for when you're amazed, songs that look at God's creation and his character and can't stop marveling.

There are psalms for when you're hurting, raw prayers from people who feel abandoned and aren't afraid to say so.

There are psalms for when you're thankful, celebrations that pour out because God answered a prayer the writer had almost given up on.

There are psalms for when you're scared, quiet declarations of trust from people who are terrified but refuse to let go.

There are psalms for when you're sorry, gut-wrenching confessions that hold nothing back.

There are psalms for when you're angry, furious prayers that ask God to bring justice on the wicked.

There are psalms for when you're trying to figure out how to live, thoughtful meditations on what it means to walk the right path when the wrong one looks easier.

There are psalms about the king who was coming, songs that dreamed of a ruler so just and powerful that only Jesus could fill the role.

There are psalms for walking together, songs pilgrims sang as they climbed the hills toward Jerusalem.

And there are psalms that look backward, retelling the story of what God has done so the next generation never forgets.

By the time you finish, you'll be able to open to any psalm in the Bible and understand what kind of song it is, what it's doing, and how to make it your own.

BEFORE YOU BEGIN

Before we start, a few things to keep in mind.

The Psalms contain some uncomfortable material. There are prayers asking God to destroy enemies in graphic terms. There are descriptions of suffering so intense they're hard to read. There are moments of doubt so raw they might surprise you, coming from people the Bible calls faithful. We won't skip over any of it. We'll talk about why it's there and what it means.

The Psalms are poetry, not prose. That means they work differently from the narrative books you may have read in this series. They use images instead of explanations. They say things twice in different words. They compress enormous ideas into single lines. Reading them requires a different pace, and we'll spend a whole chapter learning how to do it well.

And the Psalms point to Jesus. Not just a few of them. All of them. The king they hoped for, the shepherd they trusted, the deliverer they begged for, the God they praised in the dark, all of it finds its deepest meaning in Christ. He prayed these words. He fulfilled these songs. And when you pray them, you're joining a conversation that stretches from an ancient harp to the throne room of heaven.

One hundred and fifty songs. Every emotion you've ever felt and some you haven't felt yet. A God who doesn't want your polished version but your honest one. And a Christ who walked into these poems before you did, praying them from the inside, and who meets you there every time you open the book.

The Psalms have been waiting for you.

Turn the page.

1

GOD'S PLAYLIST

Riley has a problem. Actually, Riley has a lot of problems.

If you've seen *Inside Out 2*, you know what happens when Riley hits thirteen. Her emotional world, which used to be run by five familiar feelings, suddenly gets invaded by new ones. Anxiety shows up uninvited and starts running the control panel. Embarrassment lurks in the corner. Envy sneaks in. And for a while, the emotions Riley has known her whole life get shoved aside, locked away in a vault because the new feelings insist they're the ones in charge now.

Here's what makes the movie so smart: the solution isn't to get rid of the uncomfortable emotions. It's to let all of them have a voice. Joy can't run things alone. Anxiety isn't the enemy. Sadness matters. Fear has a purpose. Riley doesn't become whole by silencing the hard feelings. She becomes whole by letting every emotion be heard.

The book of Psalms works the same way.

150 SONGS, ONE BOOK

Psalms is the Bible's most emotionally honest book. It is 150 poems, prayers, and songs that cover every feeling a human being can experience. Joy. Grief. Anger. Fear. Gratitude. Loneliness. Wonder. Confusion. Guilt. Trust. Rage at enemies. Frustration with God. Quiet confidence in the dark. Explosive celebration in the light.

No other book in the Bible sounds like this. Most books tell you what happened or what God said. Psalms shows you what it feels like to believe in God when life is beautiful and when life is falling apart. It's the one place in Scripture where people say exactly what they're thinking, hold nothing back, and somehow that raw honesty becomes worship.

If the rest of the Bible is God speaking to his people, the Psalms are God's people speaking back.

THE SONGWRITERS

So who wrote all these songs? The short answer: a lot of people, over a very long time.

Nearly half the psalms are connected to David, the shepherd-turned-king you meet in 1 Samuel. And that makes sense. David was a musician before he was anything else. When we first encounter him in the Bible, he's playing a stringed instrument so beautifully that it calms King Saul's troubled mind. Later, he organized the entire worship system for Israel, appointing musicians and singers to lead the nation in praise. He called himself "the sweet singer of Israel," and the title stuck.

But David wasn't the only songwriter. A group of temple musicians called the Sons of Korah wrote at least eleven psalms. A worship leader named Asaph wrote twelve. Solomon contributed a couple. Moses wrote one, making it possibly the oldest song in the collection. And quite a few psalms have no name attached at all. They're anonymous, written by people whose names have been forgotten but whose words have echoed for three thousand years.

What all these writers had in common was this: they wrote out of real life. When they were rescued from danger, they wrote songs of thanks. When they were crushed by grief, they wrote songs of lament. When they looked at the night sky and felt small, they wrote songs of wonder. When they watched wicked people prosper while the faithful suffered, they wrote songs that wrestled honestly with the unfairness of it all.

These weren't written to sit on a shelf. They were written to be sung, out loud, in community. Imagine an ancient Israelite walking toward the temple in Jerusalem with thousands of other worshipers, singing these songs together as they climbed the hills. That's what they were made for. They were Israel's hymnal, the soundtrack of their faith.

FIVE BOOKS IN ONE

Here's something most people don't notice: the book of Psalms isn't one book. It's five.

Somewhere along the way, the editors who compiled the final collection divided the 150 psalms into five sections, called "books." Book 1 contains Psalms 1–41. Book 2 covers Psalms 42–72. Book 3 is Psalms 73–89. Book 4 runs from Psalm 90–106. And Book 5 closes things out with Psalms 107–150. Each book ends with a short burst of praise, like a period at the end of a sentence.

Why five? Most scholars think it was intentional. The first five books of the Bible, Genesis through Deuteronomy, are the foundation of everything. By dividing the Psalms into five books too, the editors were making a quiet statement: this collection of prayers deserves to be read alongside the words God spoke to his people. It's that important.

And if you open your Bible to the middle, odds are good you'll land somewhere in the Psalms. It's not just at the center of the Bible by accident. It's at the heart of the Bible because it *is* the heart of the Bible. It's where everything else comes together, not as theology or history, but as prayer.

A MIRROR FOR THE SOUL

Think about that word for a second: prayer. Most of the Bible tells you what God did. Psalms shows you how people responded to what God did. And the responses are raw. The psalmists don't clean up their language. They don't pretend to feel things they don't feel. When they're overjoyed, they shout. When they're devastated, they weep. When they're furious, they say so, sometimes in ways that make modern readers uncomfortable.

The Psalms are like a mirror for the soul. When you look into a regular mirror, you see how you look on the outside. When you read the Psalms, you see how you're doing on the inside. You might open to a psalm and think, *That's exactly how I feel.* Or you might read one and realize you've been feeling something you didn't even have words for until the psalmist handed them to you.

That's what makes this book different from anything else in Scripture. It meets you wherever you are. Celebrating? There's a psalm for that. Terrified? There's a psalm for that too. Struggling to believe God cares? There's an entire category of psalms for that, and there are more of them than any other kind.

FROM PAIN TO PRAISE

That last point matters. The largest group of psalms in the book isn't praise. It's lament. Songs of pain, confusion, and complaint. Songs where the writer looks at God and says, "How long? Have you forgotten me? Do you even see what's happening?"

If that surprises you, it shouldn't. Life is hard, and the Bible doesn't pretend otherwise. What the Psalms teach us is that bringing our pain to God isn't a failure of faith. It *is* faith. It's trusting God enough to be honest with him, even when that honesty sounds more like a scream than a prayer.

But here's what's remarkable about the book as a whole. Even though laments dominate the early psalms, the book doesn't stay there. As you move through the five books, something shifts. Praise starts showing up more and more. The complaints don't disappear, but they get surrounded by trust. By the time you reach the final five psalms, it's nothing but praise. Psalm 150 is one explosion of worship after another, every instrument playing, every voice raised.

The whole book bends toward praise. Not because the pain wasn't real, but because God was more real than the pain.

SONGS THAT WERE WAITING

One more thing before we dive in. The Psalms don't just look backward at Israel's experiences. They look forward, to someone who hadn't come yet.

When Jesus was dying on the cross, the words he cried out came from Psalm 22. When the New Testament writers wanted to explain who Jesus was, they quoted the Psalms more than almost any other book. The king the psalms hoped for, the shepherd they trusted, the rescuer they begged for, the God they praised in the dark—all of it finds its fullest meaning in Jesus.

As we walk through this book together, watch for that. The Psalms aren't just ancient songs. They're songs that were waiting for someone, and he came.

WHAT THIS MEANS FOR US

First, every emotion you feel has a place before God. You don't have to clean yourself up before you pray. You don't have to pretend to feel grateful when you're actually angry, or act brave when you're actually terrified. The Psalms prove that God doesn't want your polished version. He wants the real one. Bring him whatever you've got, even if it's messy.

Second, faith isn't the absence of hard feelings. Some of the most faith-filled people in the Bible wrote the most anguished prayers. Faith isn't pretending everything is fine. It's choosing to bring your pain to God instead of running from him. The psalmists screamed, questioned, and complained, but they always directed it toward God, not away from him.

Third, you were made for worship in community. The Psalms were written to be sung together. Faith was never meant to be a solo act. When you gather with other Christians to worship, pray, and be honest about life, you're doing exactly what these songs were designed for.

Fourth, the story always bends toward praise. Life includes seasons of grief and confusion and anger. The Psalms don't deny that. But they show us that the last word is never pain. It's praise. Not because the pain wasn't real, but because God is faithful and his love doesn't quit.

TALKING POINTS

1. **The Psalms contain more songs of pain than songs of praise.** Why do you think God included so many laments in his Word? What does that tell us about how he views our struggles?

2. **David was called "the sweet singer of Israel," and many of his psalms came out of real experiences, both good and terrible.** Why do you think music and poetry are such powerful ways to express faith? Is there a song or a piece of writing that has helped you through a hard time?

3. **The Psalms have been called a mirror for the soul.** What do you think that means? Have you ever read something in the Bible and felt like it described exactly what you were going through?

4. **The book of Psalms moves from mostly lament at the beginning to pure praise at the end.** Why do you think the editors arranged it that way? What does that movement from pain to praise teach us about the life of faith?

5. **Jesus quoted the Psalms from the cross.** What does it mean to you that even Jesus turned to these ancient songs in his darkest moment?

That's the big picture. One hundred and fifty songs. Dozens of writers. Five books. Every emotion you've ever felt and some you haven't felt yet. A sacred space made of words, sitting right at the center of your Bible, waiting for you to walk in.

The Psalms aren't just a collection. They're an invitation: to be honest, to worship, to bring everything you are before the God who made you and see what he does with it.

We're about to find out what kinds of songs are in this playlist, starting with the ones people have always loved best, the psalms that look at God and can't stop saying how amazing he is.

Turn the page.

2

HOW TO READ A SONG

When Alice tumbles down the rabbit hole in Lewis Carroll's *Alice in Wonderland*, she lands in a world where nothing works the way she expects. Cats vanish and leave their grins behind. A caterpillar sits on a mushroom asking riddles. A tea party has been going on forever because time itself got offended and stopped. Alice keeps trying to apply the rules she knows, the logic that made perfect sense back home, and none of it works. She's not in a different place. She's in a different *kind* of place, and it requires a completely different way of thinking.

Something similar happens when you've been reading the story-driven books of the Bible and then open to the Psalms. If you've been following along through Genesis, Exodus, Joshua, and 1 Samuel, you've been reading narratives. Stories with characters and plots and beginnings and endings. You know how those work. You follow the action, track the people, and see what happens next.

Then you hit Psalms, and the rules change.

There's no plot. No characters doing things in order. Instead, there are lines that seem to say the same thing twice.

Images pile up without explanation. God is called a rock in one line and a shield in the next and a fortress two lines later. If you try to read a psalm the way you read a story, it will feel repetitive, confusing, and flat.

But it's not flat. You're just in a different kind of place. And once you learn how this place works, it comes alive.

A DIFFERENT KIND OF WRITING

Every psalm in the book is a poem. That's the first thing to understand. You're not reading history or law or a letter. You're reading poetry, and poetry plays by its own rules.

You can actually see the difference just by looking at the page. Open your Bible to a chapter in 1 Samuel, and you'll see solid paragraphs of text running from margin to margin, just like a novel. Now flip to a psalm. The text looks completely different. Short lines. Lots of white space. Pairs of phrases stacked on top of each other. It almost looks like song lyrics, and that's exactly what it is.

Poetry compresses language. A story might take a whole paragraph to describe how someone feels. A poem does it in a single image. A story gives you details and explanations. A poem gives you a picture and trusts you to sit with it. Less is more. Every word carries weight.

That means you can't speed through a psalm the way you might speed through a story. Stories pull you forward. You want to know what happens next. Poems ask you to slow down. Read the line. Read it again. Let the image settle. The meaning isn't hiding from you, but it does unfold more slowly than a plot does.

SAYING IT TWICE

Here's the feature of the Psalms that confuses people most: the poets keep saying things twice. Look at Psalm 19:1:

> The heavens declare the glory of God;
>> the skies proclaim the work of his hands.

"The heavens" and "the skies" are basically the same thing. "Declare the glory of God" and "proclaim the work of his hands" are making the same point. So why say it twice? Is the poet just filling space?

Not even close. This is the most important technique in all of biblical poetry. Scholars call it **parallelism**, and it shows up in almost every line of every psalm. Two phrases are placed side by side, and they echo each other, but they're never just repeating. The second line always does something to the first. It sharpens it, intensifies it, or pushes the thought further.

Go back to that verse. "The heavens declare the glory of God" is a big, sweeping statement. Then the second line narrows the focus: "the skies proclaim the work of his hands." It moves from God's glory in general to his *craftsmanship* in particular. You go from "God is glorious" to "look at what he made." The camera zooms in.

Here's another example. Psalm 42:1:

> As the deer pants for flowing streams,
>> so my soul pants for you, O God.

The first line gives you a picture: an exhausted deer, desperate for water. The second line tells you what the picture means: *that's how I feel about God*. The first line sets up the image. The second line lands the punch.

Once you start watching for this, you'll see it everywhere. And it changes how you read. Instead of thinking *he just said the same thing twice*, start asking: *What did the second line add? How did it sharpen the first one? Where did the thought go?*

That's how you read a psalm.

PICTURES, NOT DEFINITIONS

The second thing to know about the Psalms is that they run on imagery. The poets don't describe God the way a textbook would. They don't say, "God is powerful and protective." They say, "God is my rock, my fortress, and my deliverer" (Psalm 18:2). They don't say, "God takes care of me." They say, "The LORD is my shepherd" (Psalm 23:1).

These are metaphors, and they're everywhere in the Psalms. God is a rock. A shield. A fortress. A king. A warrior. A shepherd. A mother bird gathering her young under her wings. Each image reveals something true about God, but none of them gives you the whole picture. God isn't literally made of stone. He doesn't literally carry a shield. But when you're terrified and you need to know that God is unshakable, "rock" says it better than any definition could.

The poets don't limit their imagery to God, either. Enemies are described as lions, dogs, and swarming bees. The righteous person is a tree planted by streams of water. The wicked are chaff, the dry husks that blow away when the wind comes. A guilty conscience is described as bones wasting away. Joy is described as a cup overflowing.

These images aren't decoration. They're the *point*. The poet chose that picture because it captures something that plain language can't. When Psalm 42 says, "Deep calls to deep in the roar of your waterfalls; all your waves and breakers have swept over me," the writer isn't talking about actual water. He's drowning in grief, and he wants you to feel it in your chest, not just understand it in your head.

That's what poetry does. It doesn't just inform your brain. It gets into your gut.

READING SLOW

So how should you actually read a psalm? Here are three habits that will change everything.

First, read it more than once. A story works fine on a single pass. A poem doesn't. Read the whole psalm through once to get the feel of it. Then go back and read it again, line by line. Watch how the second half of each line builds on the first. Notice which images show up. Ask yourself what the poet is feeling and why.

Second, pay attention to the pictures. When you hit a metaphor, don't skip past it. Stop and think about it. If the psalmist says God is a shield, what does that mean? What does a shield actually do? It puts itself between you and whatever's trying to hurt you. Now you're not just reading a word. You're seeing something.

Third, put yourself in the poem. The Psalms were written so that anyone could pray them. When you read "my soul pants for you, O God," don't just think about the original author. Ask yourself: *Is that how I feel? Have I ever felt that way? What would it take for me to mean those words?* The Psalms aren't meant to be studied from a distance. They're meant to be prayed from the inside.

WHAT THIS MEANS FOR US

First, slowing down is not a waste of time. We live in a world that moves fast. We scroll, skim, and skip. The Psalms push back against all of that. They reward the person who reads carefully, who sits with a single verse and lets it unfold. Some of the deepest truths in the Bible are buried in two-line poems that you could read in three seconds or think about for three years.

Second, not everything true can be said in a straight line. Some things are better expressed through pictures than through explanations. When you're scared and someone tells you "God is in control," that's true. But when a poet says "God is my refuge and strength, a very present help in trouble" (Psalm 46:1), something different happens. You don't just hear the idea. You feel the shelter. Poetry reaches places that plain statements can't.

Third, the Bible isn't just a book of information. It's a book that's trying to change you. The Psalms don't just teach you facts about God. They stir your emotions, fire your imagination, and call you to respond. God didn't give us 150 poems because he ran out of ways to say things in prose. He gave us poetry because some truths need to be felt, not just known.

Fourth, learning to read well is an act of worship. When you slow down, pay attention to the images, and let a psalm sink into your heart, you're not just doing homework. You're entering the space where God's people have met him for over three thousand years. You're joining the conversation. And the better you listen, the more you'll hear.

TALKING POINTS

1. **Most of the Bible is written as narrative. The Psalms are written as poetry, which follows completely different rules.** What's the difference between reading a story and reading a poem? Which one do you find easier, and why? How might the Psalms change the way you read the Bible?

2. **Parallelism means the second line of a pair always adds something to the first. Pick one of the examples from this chapter and explain in your own words what the second line adds.** Why do you think the poet didn't just say it once?

3. **The Psalms describe God as a rock, a shield, a shepherd, a fortress, and a mother bird.** Which of those images means the most to you right now, and why? What does that image show you about God that a plain statement wouldn't?

4. **This chapter suggests reading a psalm more than once and reading slowly.** Why is that hard to do in our culture? What habits could you build to help you slow down when you're reading Scripture?

5. **The Bible includes poetry, not just stories and laws.** Why do you think God chose to communicate some truths through poems and songs instead of straightforward explanations? What can poetry do that prose can't?

Now you have the tools. You know what to watch for when you read a psalm: lines that echo and build, images that paint instead of explain, and a pace that rewards patience instead of speed. You know you're in a different kind of place, and you know how to move through it.

It's time to step into the songs themselves. And we're starting with the psalms that sound like the whole world is singing, the ones that look at who God is and what he's made and can barely contain the joy.

Turn the page.

3

WHEN YOU'RE AMAZED

There's a scene early in *Bambi* that doesn't have any dialogue, any villain, or any danger. It's just a young deer stepping out of the forest into a meadow for the first time. And somehow, it's one of the most memorable moments in the entire film.

Up until that point, Bambi's world has been small. Trees close together. Shadows everywhere. A few familiar faces. Then his mother leads him out into the open, and suddenly the world is enormous. The meadow stretches out in every direction, bathed in light. Butterflies lift off the grass. The sky goes on forever. Bambi doesn't know what to do with it. He just stands there, taking it in, overwhelmed by something he didn't know existed.

That moment captures something the Bible talks about a lot: the experience of looking at the world God made and being completely, speechlessly amazed.

The Psalms have a whole category of songs for that feeling. Scholars call them hymns or praise psalms. They're the songs people wrote when they looked up at the night sky, or watched the sun race across the horizon, or thought about how vast and powerful God is, and couldn't keep quiet about it. They didn't sit down and write a theology paper. They sang.

THE GOD WHO DESERVES A STANDING OVATION

Praise psalms are the most joyful songs in the book. They're not asking God for anything. They're not working through a problem. They're not confessing sin or processing pain. They're doing one thing: celebrating who God is and what he's done.

Most of them follow a simple pattern. They open with a call to worship, something like "Praise the Lord!" or "Sing to the Lord a new song!" Then they give the reasons: *this* is why God deserves praise. And many of them close with another burst of worship, as if the poet just can't stop.

That structure might sound repetitive, but it's actually what joy does. Think about it. When something amazing happens, you don't say it once and move on. You tell everyone. You repeat yourself. You circle back to it hours later and say, "Can you believe that?" The praise psalms sound like someone who has seen something so incredible that one round of applause isn't enough.

Three psalms in particular show what this looks like, and each one takes the praise in a slightly different direction.

PSALM 8: SMALL AND SIGNIFICANT

Psalm 8 starts and ends with the same line: "O LORD, our Lord, how majestic is your name in all the earth!" That frame tells you the whole psalm is about one thing: God's majesty.

But here's where it gets interesting. The psalmist isn't praising God for military victories or answered prayers. He's outside at night, looking up. "When I consider your heavens, the work of your fingers, the moon and the stars, which you have set in place, what is mankind that you are mindful of them, human beings that you care for them?"

Did you catch the emotional shift? He starts with wonder at the sky and lands on a question: *Why would the God who made all of that care about us?* The stars are enormous, ancient, and countless. Humans are tiny by comparison. We live on a small planet in a vast universe. When you actually stop and think about the scale of what God created, the obvious question is why he would pay any attention to people at all.

And then the psalm answers its own question. Instead of saying humans are insignificant, it says the opposite. God made them "a little lower than the heavenly beings" and "crowned them with glory and honor." He gave them authority over the rest of creation: the animals, the birds, the fish, everything. The God who flung the stars into space looked at human beings and said, "You are my masterpiece. I'm putting you in charge."

That's the genius of Psalm 8. It holds two feelings at the same time. Smallness and significance. You look at the night sky and feel tiny. Then you realize the God who made that sky knows your name, chose you, and crowned you with purpose. Both things are true. You are small in the universe. And you matter enormously to the God who made it.

The New Testament takes this even further. The author of Hebrews quotes Psalm 8 and applies it to Jesus, the one who was made "a little lower than the angels" for a time but is now crowned with glory and honor because of his suffering and death. In other words, Jesus is the ultimate answer to the psalm's question. Why does God care about humanity? Because he became one of us.

PSALM 19: THE SKY THAT WON'T STOP TALKING

Psalm 19 picks up a theme that Psalm 8 only hinted at and turns it into one of the most beautiful poems in the Bible. "The heavens declare the glory of God; the skies proclaim the work of his hands. Day after day they pour forth speech; night after night they reveal knowledge."

Creation is talking. Not with words, not with sound, but with something you can't ignore if you're paying attention. Every sunrise, every thunderstorm, every star-filled night is saying the same thing: *Someone made this. Someone powerful, creative, and beautiful stands behind all of it.*

The psalm says this speech goes out to the whole world. "There is no speech or language where their voice is not heard. Their voice goes out into all the earth." You don't have to speak a certain language to get the message. You don't need a degree. You just need eyes. Creation is God's first sermon, and it never stops preaching.

Then the psalm shifts. The poet moves from creation to God's Word, his law. And he praises it with the same enthusiasm he used for the night sky: "The law of the LORD is perfect, refreshing the soul. The statutes of the LORD are trustworthy, making wise the simple." He calls God's words more precious than gold and sweeter than honey.

Why put those two things together, creation and Scripture? Because both of them reveal who God is. The sky shows you his power and beauty. His Word shows you his character, his will, and his heart. One speaks without words. The other speaks with words. And together, they give you a picture of God that takes your breath away.

The psalm ends with a prayer: "May these words of my mouth and this meditation of my heart be pleasing in your sight, LORD, my Rock and my Redeemer." After everything he's seen in the sky and read in God's law, the psalmist turns inward. He wants his own life to be as beautiful as the things he's been praising. That's what real worship does. It doesn't just admire God from a distance. It makes you want to live differently.

PSALM 148: EVERYTHING, EVERYWHERE, ALL AT ONCE

If Psalm 8 is one person standing under the stars and Psalm 19 is the sky delivering a silent sermon, then Psalm 148 is the moment the entire universe joins the choir.

This psalm doesn't ease into things. It starts with a command and never lets up: "Praise the LORD from the heavens; praise him in the heights above. Praise him, all his angels; praise him, all his heavenly hosts."

Then it works its way down through creation, calling on everything to worship. Sun and moon. Stars. The highest heavens. Then it drops to earth. Sea creatures. Lightning and hail. Snow and clouds. Mountains and hills. Fruit trees and cedars. Wild animals and cattle. Small creatures and flying birds. Kings and princes. Young men and young women. Old people and children.

Everyone. Everything. No exceptions.

Psalm 148 doesn't give reasons for each group. It doesn't explain why the mountains should praise God or how the sea creatures would do it. It doesn't need to. The point isn't the mechanics. The point is that nothing in all creation should be silent when it comes to praising the God who made it. Existence itself is a reason to worship.

The psalm ends by narrowing from the whole cosmos to one specific group: God's people. "He has raised up for his people a horn, the praise of all his faithful servants, of Israel, the people close to his heart." Everyone should praise God because he's the Creator. But God's people have a special reason. He hasn't just made them. He's close to them. He's chosen them, rescued them, and stayed with them.

If you've ever been to a concert where the whole crowd is singing along, you have a tiny glimpse of what Psalm 148 is imagining. Except the crowd includes angels and ocean waves and thunderstorms and pine trees. The psalm is picturing the entire universe doing what it was made to do: worship the God who made it.

WHAT THIS MEANS FOR US

First, praise is the most natural thing in the world. We were made for it. When you see a sunset that stops you in your tracks, or stand at the edge of the ocean and feel small, that impulse to say "wow" is built into you. The praise psalms are just what happens when someone lets that impulse run all the way to God.

Second, creation is still speaking. You don't have to live in ancient Israel to hear it. The same sky that spoke to the psalmist three thousand years ago is above you right now. Pay attention. Put your phone down. Go outside. Let the world preach to you.

Third, you are small and you are significant. Those two things aren't contradictions. Psalm 8 holds them together, and so should you. The universe is incomprehensibly vast, and the God who made it knows your name, hears your voice, and crowned you with purpose. Never let the size of the universe make you forget the size of God's love for you.

Fourth, worship is meant to be shared. Psalm 148 doesn't picture a single voice. It pictures everything that exists joining in. When you worship with other Christians, you're participating in something that's happening everywhere, all the time, across the entire created order. You're adding your voice to a chorus that started before you were born and will continue long after you're gone.

TALKING POINTS

1. **Psalm 8 says looking at the night sky makes the psalmist wonder why God would care about humans.** Have you ever had a moment in nature where you felt very small? What did that feel like, and how did it affect the way you think about God?

2. **Psalm 19 says creation "pours forth speech" without using words.** What do you think that means? What has creation "said" to you about God?

3. **The psalmist in Psalm 19 moves from praising creation to praising God's Word, and then to examining his own heart.** Why do you think praise leads to self-reflection? How does worshiping God change the way you see yourself?

4. **Psalm 148 calls on everything in creation to praise God, from angels to sea creatures to snowstorms.** Why do

you think the poet includes things that can't literally sing? What would it look like for creation to "praise" God?

5. **These psalms were written thousands of years ago, but they describe feelings people still have today when they encounter something beautiful or awe-inspiring.** Why do you think the experience of wonder and amazement has stayed the same across all that time?

The praise psalms are the brightest songs in the book. They're full of joy, wonder, and celebration. If the Psalms were a playlist, these would be the songs you listen to on a clear day with the windows down.

But life isn't always a clear day. Sometimes the sky is dark and the only honest thing you can say to God is "I'm hurting." The psalmists knew that feeling too, and they didn't stay quiet about it.

Turn the page.

4

WHEN YOU'RE HURTING

Halfway through Johanna Spyri's novel *Heidi*, something terrible happens to a little girl who loves the mountains. Heidi is taken from her grandfather's cabin in the Swiss Alps, the only place she has ever felt truly at home, and sent to live in Frankfurt with a wealthy family. The city is supposed to be an improvement. Better food. Better education. A nicer life.

But Heidi doesn't get better. She gets worse. The walls close in. The noise never stops. She can't see the mountains. She can't hear the wind. She stops eating. She starts sleepwalking, opening the front door in the middle of the night and standing there, asleep, as if her body is trying to go home without her. She doesn't just miss the mountains. She aches for them so deeply it's making her sick.

That kind of longing, the kind that sits in your chest and won't let go, is exactly what the largest group of psalms in the Bible sounds like. They're called laments, and they're the songs people wrote when God felt as far away as a mountain you can't get back to.

THE SONGS NOBODY TEACHES YOU

Here's something strange: even though laments make up the biggest category of psalms in the entire book, most people have never been taught how to read one. Sunday school classes tend to focus on the cheerful psalms. "The Lord is my shepherd." "This is the day the Lord has made." Nobody puts Psalm 13 on a coffee mug.

But the Bible didn't accidentally include more laments than any other type of song. It included them on purpose, because life hurts more often than we like to admit, and God wanted his people to know they could bring that pain straight to him.

A lament isn't just complaining. It's a prayer with a shape. Most laments follow a pattern: the writer cries out to God, describes the pain, asks for help, and then, even in the middle of the darkness, finds something to hold on to. The complaint leads somewhere. It doesn't end in hopelessness. It ends in trust, sometimes barely, sometimes powerfully, but it moves.

Three laments in particular show what this looks like, and each one takes the pain deeper.

PSALM 13: HOW LONG?

Psalm 13 is one of the shortest psalms in the Bible. Six verses. That's it. But those six verses land like a hammer.

The psalm opens with a question that gets repeated four times in two verses: "How long, LORD? Will you forget me forever? How long will you hide your face from me? How long must I wrestle with my thoughts and day after day have sorrow in my heart? How long will my enemy triumph over me?"

Four times. *How long?* The psalmist isn't asking why. He's asking *when will this end?* He believes God has turned away from him, and the silence is unbearable. His mind is in turmoil. His heart is full of sorrow. And on top of everything, his enemies are winning.

Then, in verses 3–4, the tone shifts from question to demand. "Look on me and answer, LORD my God. Give light to my eyes, or I will sleep in death." He's not being polite. He's telling God: if you don't act, I'm going to die, and my enemies will celebrate. He's essentially saying, "You don't want that, do you?"

And then the ending. After all that anguish, the final two verses say this: "But I trust in your unfailing love; my heart rejoices in your salvation. I will sing the LORD's praise, for he has been good to me."

Wait. What just happened? He went from "Have you forgotten me?" to "I trust your unfailing love" in the space of six verses. Nothing in the psalm tells us his circumstances changed. No rescue showed up between verse 4 and verse 5. The psalmist simply chose, in the middle of his pain, to trust that God's love was bigger than the silence.

That's lament. Not pretending the pain isn't real. Not waiting until everything is fine to worship. Choosing trust while you're still in the dark.

PSALM 22: FORSAKEN

If Psalm 13 is a sharp cry, Psalm 22 is a long scream. "My God, my God, why have you forsaken me? Why are you so far from saving me, so far from my cries of anguish?"

You probably recognize those words. Jesus said them from the cross. But before they were the words of Jesus, they were the words of a man who felt completely abandoned by God, surrounded by enemies who mocked his faith and tore him apart.

The psalm gets worse before it gets better. The writer describes himself as "a worm and not a man, scorned by everyone, despised by the people." His enemies circle him like bulls. They're compared to roaring lions. His strength is gone, his mouth is dry, his bones stick out. People stare at him and divide up his clothing.

Read that last detail again. Divide up his clothing. A thousand years before Jesus was born, a poet wrote about enemies dividing up a sufferer's clothes. When the Roman soldiers did exactly that at the foot of the cross, the Gospel writers recognized it immediately.

But here's what most people miss about Psalm 22: it doesn't end in despair. Starting at verse 22, everything changes. The psalmist says, "I will declare your name to my brothers and sisters; in the assembly I will sing your praises." He goes from "Why have you forsaken me?" to "I will praise you in front of everyone." And the praise keeps expanding: from the psalmist to the congregation, from Israel to all nations, from the present to future generations.

The psalm starts in the darkest possible place and ends with the widest possible praise. And that's exactly what happened with Jesus. He cried out on the cross, abandoned and dying, but three days later God raised him from the dead. The psalm's pattern became Jesus' story: agony first, then glory.

PSALM 42: THIRSTY FOR GOD

Psalm 42 opens with one of the most famous images in the Bible: "As the deer pants for flowing streams, so my soul pants for you, O God. My soul thirsts for God, for the living God. When can I go and meet with God?"

This isn't gentle longing. This is desperation. The image is of an animal that will die without water. That's how badly the psalmist needs God.

The problem isn't just emotional. The writer seems to be physically separated from the temple, the place where God made his presence known in a special way. He's far from home, far from worship, far from the community that used to surround him. He remembers what it was like to worship with the crowds during the festivals, and the memory makes the present hurt worse.

To make things harder, the people around him keep asking the same question: "Where is your God?" It's a taunt. If God really cared about you, they're saying, wouldn't he be here? Wouldn't things be different?

And then the psalmist does something remarkable. He talks to himself. Three times in this psalm and the next (Psalms 42 and 43 were probably one poem originally), he repeats the same refrain: "Why, my soul, are you downcast? Why so disturbed within me? Put your hope in God, for I will yet praise him, my Savior and my God."

He doesn't argue with his feelings. He doesn't deny that he's downcast. But he refuses to let his feelings have the last word. He preaches to himself. He tells his own soul to hope, even when nothing around him supports that hope. It's not a triumphant declaration. It's more like someone gripping a rope in the dark, whispering, "Don't let go."

THE SHAPE OF A LAMENT

Did you notice the pattern? All three psalms do the same thing, even though the details are different.

They cry out. They describe the pain honestly. They ask God for help. And then they land, however shakily, on trust. The pain doesn't disappear. The circumstances don't magically change. But the psalmist moves, inch by inch, from complaint toward confidence that God hasn't actually left.

That pattern matters. It means lament isn't just venting. It's a journey. You start where you are, in the mess, in the tears, in the anger, and you walk toward God through it. You don't have to arrive at perfect peace by the last verse. The psalmist in Psalm 42 is still telling himself to hope at the end, not declaring that everything is fine. But he's moving. And the movement itself is faith.

WHAT THIS MEANS FOR US

First, God can handle your honesty. The psalmists didn't filter their prayers. They said "How long?" and "Why have you forsaken me?" and "Where are you?" These aren't rebellious questions. They're the prayers of people who trusted God enough to tell him the truth. You can do the same. God isn't offended by your pain. He's offended when you pretend it doesn't exist.

Second, feeling abandoned by God doesn't mean you are abandoned by God. Every one of these psalmists felt like God was far away. Every one of them was wrong. God hadn't left.

He was listening even when he was silent. The feeling of absence is real, but it isn't the whole truth.

Third, it's okay if trust comes slowly. Psalm 42 doesn't end with a shout of victory. It ends with a whisper of hope. That's enough. You don't have to leap from grief to praise in one breath. Faith isn't a switch you flip. Sometimes it's a direction you face, one step at a time, even when everything in you wants to sit down and quit.

Fourth, Jesus knows what this feels like. He quoted Psalm 22 from the cross. He felt the full weight of abandonment so that you would never have to face it alone. When you pray a lament, you're praying words that your Savior already prayed. He's been where you are.

TALKING POINTS

1. **Psalm 13 asks "How long?" four times in two verses.** Why do you think the psalmist repeated the question so many times? Have you ever felt that way about something in your life?

2. **Psalm 22 starts with total despair and ends with expanding praise.** What do you think caused the shift? How can someone go from feeling abandoned to worshiping God?

3. **The psalmist in Psalm 42 talks to himself, telling his own soul to hope.** Have you ever had to "preach to yourself" in a hard moment? What did that look like?

4. **These psalms are honest about pain, but they always direct that honesty toward God rather than away from him.** What's the difference between complaining to God and just complaining? Why does it matter where you aim your pain?

5. Jesus quoted Psalm 22 from the cross. How does knowing that Jesus prayed these same words change the way you read them? Does it help to know that even Jesus experienced the feeling of being abandoned by God?

Laments are the songs you sing in the dark. But they're not the only songs for hard times. Sometimes the darkness lifts, not because the pain disappears, but because you suddenly remember who God has been before. You remember what he's done. And that memory gives you enough to hold on.

The next kind of psalm is for those moments when holding on turns into giving thanks, when the prayer God answered becomes the song you can't stop singing.

Turn the page.

5

WHEN YOU'RE THANKFUL

There's a moment near the end of *One Hundred and One Dalmatians* that hits differently once you know what it took to get there. Pongo and Perdita have their puppies back. All of them. Every single spotted little body is accounted for, along with dozens more they rescued along the way. The house is full of barking and chaos and joy.

But the reason that scene feels so good is because of everything that came before it. Cruella de Vil stole the puppies. The parents were frantic. The whole network of dogs across England passed along the alert, barking through the night. Pongo and Perdita fought through blizzards and outsmarted villains and nearly lost everything. The reunion isn't just happy. It's relieved, exhausted, grateful, overwhelmed kind of happy. The kind of joy that only makes sense when you know how close things came to falling apart.

That's exactly how thanksgiving psalms work. They're not just cheerful songs about how good God is. They're the songs people sang *after* the crisis, after the lament, after they had begged God for help and he actually showed up. The joy in these psalms is so intense precisely because the pain that came before it was real.

THE OTHER SIDE OF LAMENT

Thanksgiving psalms and praise psalms might sound similar on the surface. Both celebrate God. Both are full of joy. But there's a key difference, and understanding it changes how you read both types.

Praise psalms celebrate who God is. They look at his character, his creation, his power, and they marvel. You don't need something specific to have happened. You just need to pay attention to who God is, and the praise pours out.

Thanksgiving psalms celebrate what God *did*. Something specific happened. The psalmist was in trouble, he cried out, God rescued him, and now he's telling the story. There's always a "before" and an "after." There's always a lament lurking in the background, a prayer that was finally answered.

Think of it this way. If praise is looking at God and saying, "You're amazing," thanksgiving is looking at God and saying, "You saved me, and I will never stop talking about it."

The Psalms are full of both. But thanksgiving psalms have a special energy, because you can hear the relief in them. You can hear the person remembering what it felt like to be in the dark, and marveling that the light came back.

PSALM 30: WAILING INTO DANCING

Psalm 30 is a textbook thanksgiving song. The psalmist had been seriously ill, so close to death that he described it as being pulled out of the depths like a bucket hauled up from a well.

His enemies were watching, waiting for him to die. And he cried out to God in desperation.

God answered. He healed the psalmist, and the psalmist can barely contain himself. The psalm opens with a burst of praise: "I will exalt you, LORD, for you lifted me out of the depths and did not let my enemies gloat over me."

But the psalm doesn't just celebrate the rescue. It also tells the story of what went wrong. Before the illness, the psalmist had grown comfortable. "When I felt secure, I said, 'I will never be shaken.'" He got overconfident. He forgot that his stability depended on God, not on himself. Then God "hid his face," and everything fell apart.

That's an honest confession, and it sits right in the middle of a thanksgiving song. The psalmist isn't pretending he was an innocent victim. He's admitting that his pride played a role in what happened. And that makes the gratitude even deeper, because he's not just thankful for healing. He's thankful that God loved him enough to shake him out of his self-sufficiency.

The most memorable line comes near the end: "You turned my wailing into dancing; you removed my sackcloth and clothed me with joy." Sackcloth was the rough fabric people wore during mourning. The image is vivid: God literally stripped the grief off his back and dressed him in celebration. The crisis wasn't erased. It was *transformed*. The same man who wailed is now dancing, and the dance means more because of the wailing that came first.

Then the psalmist does something every thanksgiving psalm does. He tells other people. "Sing the praises of the LORD, you his faithful people; praise his holy name." His rescue isn't a private experience. It becomes a public testimony that invites the whole community to worship.

PSALM 107: FOUR RESCUE STORIES

Psalm 107 takes the thanksgiving idea and multiplies it. Instead of one person's story, it tells four.

The psalm opens with a command: "Give thanks to the LORD, for he is good; his love endures forever. Let the redeemed of the LORD tell their story." Then it delivers exactly that, four groups of people who found themselves in desperate situations and were rescued by God.

The first group wandered in the desert, hungry, thirsty, and lost, with no city to call home. They cried out, and God led them to a place where they could settle and live.

The second group sat in prison, locked up in darkness and chains. Their imprisonment was the consequence of their own rebellion against God. But when they cried out, he broke their chains and brought them into the light.

The third group had become fools through their sin. Their rebellion made them sick, and they were wasting away. But when they cried out, God sent his word and healed them.

The fourth group were sailors caught in a terrifying storm. The waves tossed their ships. Their courage melted. They were at the end of their wits. And when they cried out, God stilled the storm and guided them safely to harbor.

Did you notice the pattern? Every single group hits the same crisis point: *then they cried out to the LORD in their trouble.* And every single time, God responds: *and he delivered them from their distress.* After each rescue, the psalm repeats the same refrain: "Let them give thanks to the LORD for his unfailing love and his wonderful deeds for mankind."

Four stories. One pattern. Trouble. Cry. Rescue. Thanks.

The psalm is making a point that goes beyond any single rescue. It's saying this is what God *does*. This is who he is. He hears desperate people and he acts. Your specific crisis might look like a desert or a prison or a storm, but the God who answers is the same every time.

PSALM 136: THE REFRAIN THAT NEVER STOPS

Psalm 136 is unlike anything else in the book. Every single verse, all twenty-six of them, ends with the same phrase: "His love endures forever."

This wasn't just a literary choice. It was a worship experience. In the temple, the worship leader would sing the first half of each verse, and the entire congregation would respond with the refrain. Back and forth, twenty-six times. It was a call-and-response that built like a wave.

The content moves through the whole sweep of God's story. It starts with creation: he made the heavens, spread out the earth, set the sun and moon in place. His love endures forever. Then it moves to the exodus: he struck down Egypt's firstborn, brought Israel out, divided the sea, led them through the wilderness. His love endures forever. Then the conquest: he defeated kings and gave his people a land to call their own. His love endures forever. And it closes with a summary: he remembered his people when they were at their lowest and rescued them from their enemies. His love endures forever.

The repetition is the point. When you say the same phrase twenty-six times, it stops being just a statement and becomes a drumbeat. It gets under your skin. It rewires how you see everything. Creation? That's love. The exodus? That's love. Your rescue, your provision, your breath today? That's love. The same love. The love that doesn't stop.

For Christians, the story doesn't end with the Old Testament. God's love endured all the way to a cross, where his Son died so that his people could be rescued one final time. His love endures forever.

WHAT THIS MEANS FOR US

First, remembering is an act of worship. The thanksgiving psalms don't forget the trouble. They retell it on purpose, because the rescue only makes sense against the backdrop of the crisis. When you remember what God brought you through, you're not dwelling on the past. You're building a case for trusting him in the future.

Second, your story is meant to be shared. Every thanksgiving psalm goes public. The psalmist doesn't just thank God privately. He gathers the community and says, "Let me tell you what God did." Your experiences of God's faithfulness aren't just for you. They're fuel for someone else's faith.

Third, thanksgiving follows lament. If you're in the middle of a lament right now, a thanksgiving psalm is where the story is headed. The pain may not be over yet, but these psalms show you what's on the other side. God hears. God acts. And the day is coming when your wailing will become dancing.

Fourth, God's love doesn't have an expiration date. Psalm 136 says it twenty-six times because once isn't enough. His love endured through creation, through the exodus, through exile, through the cross, and it endures right now, for you. It doesn't run out. It doesn't wear thin. It endures forever.

TALKING POINTS

1. **Psalm 30 says the psalmist grew overconfident before his crisis.** Have you ever felt so comfortable that you stopped depending on God? What happened?

2. **Psalm 107 tells four different rescue stories that all follow the same pattern.** Why do you think the psalm repeats the same structure four times? What is it trying to teach us about how God works?

3. **The thanksgiving psalms always include the hard part of the story, the trouble that came before the rescue.** Why is it important to remember the pain, not just the relief? How does remembering the crisis deepen your gratitude?

4. **Psalm 136 repeats "his love endures forever" twenty-six times.** What effect does that kind of repetition have on you? Have you ever had a truth about God that you needed to hear over and over before it sank in?

5. **These psalms all involve telling other people what God has done.** Is there a time when hearing someone else's story of God's faithfulness encouraged you? Is there a story from your own life that you could share with someone?

Thanksgiving psalms are the sound of someone on the other side. The storm passed. The chains broke. The sickness lifted.

And the first thing they did was open their mouth and tell everyone what God had done.

But not every psalm is about looking back at what God did. Some are about looking around at what God is doing right now, in the moment, when everything is dark and you need to know he's still there. Those are the songs for people who aren't celebrating yet. They're just holding on.

Turn the page.

6

WHEN YOU'RE SCARED

Early in *The Swiss Family Robinson*, a family is shipwrecked on an uninhabited island. The storm that destroyed their ship was violent. The rest of the crew fled in lifeboats without them. When the family finally makes it to shore, they have almost nothing: no map, no neighbors, no idea what's out there in the jungle. They're alone in an unfamiliar place, surrounded by wild animals and unknown dangers, with no rescue on the horizon.

But the father doesn't panic. He assesses what they have. He builds a shelter from what the wreckage provides. He leads the family inland to find water, food, and safer ground. Step by step, the island that terrified them becomes a place where they can live. Not because the dangers disappeared, but because they found refuge in the middle of them.

The Psalms have a whole category of songs that do something similar. They're called psalms of confidence, or psalms of trust, and they're written by people who are very much aware of the danger around them. Enemies are closing in. The ground is shaking. Death feels close. But instead of running or falling apart, these psalmists grab hold of one truth and refuse to let go: God is here, and that changes everything.

NOT THE ABSENCE OF FEAR

Here's the important thing to understand about trust psalms. They're not written by people who aren't afraid. They're written by people who are terrified but have decided to trust God anyway.

That distinction matters. If these were songs from people lounging in safety, they wouldn't mean much. Anyone can feel brave when nothing is wrong. What makes these psalms powerful is that the danger is real, the threat is present, and the psalmist chooses trust in the middle of it.

These aren't the same as the praise psalms, which celebrate God's greatness from a position of joy. And they're not the same as the laments, which pour out raw pain and beg God to act. Trust psalms sit somewhere in between. The pain is real, but the response isn't a scream. It's a quiet, deliberate grip on God's character, a decision to believe that who God is matters more than what the circumstances look like.

Three psalms show this better than any others.

PSALM 23: THROUGH THE VALLEY

Psalm 23 is the most famous psalm in the Bible. Even people who don't read the Bible know the opening line: "The LORD is my shepherd, I shall not want."

The shepherd metaphor isn't just pastoral. It's royal. In the ancient world, kings were called shepherds of their people. When the psalmist calls God his shepherd, he's saying, "The King of the universe is personally responsible for me."

And under that kind of care, the sheep has everything it needs. Green pastures. Quiet waters. Right paths. Rest.

But here's where most people misread the psalm. They think it's describing a life without problems. It isn't. Look at verse 4: "Even though I walk through the darkest valley, I will fear no evil, for you are with me; your rod and your staff, they comfort me."

The path goes *through* the valley, not around it. The shepherd doesn't eliminate the danger. He walks through it with you. The darkness is real. The valley is real. But so is the presence of the One walking beside you, carrying a rod to fight off predators and a staff to pull you back when you wander.

Then comes verse 5, and the metaphor shifts. God isn't just a shepherd anymore. He's a host at a banquet: "You prepare a table before me in the presence of my enemies." This isn't a quiet, private dinner. The enemies are right there, watching, and God is pouring the wine and anointing the psalmist's head with oil as if to say, "You are my honored guest, and I am not worried about them."

The psalm ends with one of the most beautiful lines in Scripture: "Surely goodness and love will follow me all the days of my life, and I will dwell in the house of the LORD forever." The word "follow" could also be translated "pursue." God's goodness and love don't just trail quietly behind you. They chase you down. They hunt you through every valley, every shadow, and every hard road.

Jesus called himself the Good Shepherd (John 10:11), the one who "lays down his life for the sheep." Psalm 23 was waiting for him.

PSALM 46: WHEN THE EARTH GIVES WAY

Psalm 46 starts with a bold declaration: "God is our refuge and strength, an ever-present help in trouble."

Then it describes the kind of trouble that makes most declarations feel hollow: "Therefore we will not fear, though the earth give way and the mountains fall into the heart of the sea, though its waters roar and foam and the mountains quake with their surging."

This isn't a metaphor for a bad day. This is the ground beneath your feet dissolving. Mountains, the most permanent and unmovable things the ancient world could imagine, crumbling into the ocean. If mountains can fall, nothing is safe. Everything you thought was solid is suddenly unstable.

And the psalmist says: *we will not fear.* Not because the danger isn't real, but because God is a refuge. That word means a place you run to when everything else is collapsing. You don't build a refuge. You find one. And God is already there.

The middle of the psalm shifts to a picture of a city with a river running through it, representing God's presence. While nations rage and kingdoms fall, God speaks one word and the earth melts. He's not scrambling to keep up with the chaos. He's in control of it.

Then comes verse 10, one of the most misunderstood lines in the book: "Be still, and know that I am God."

People like to put that on bookmarks and coffee mugs, as if it's a gentle suggestion to relax. It's not. In context, God is addressing the nations that are raging against him. "Be still" is closer to "Stop fighting. Stand down. I am God, and you are not." It's a command from the King of the universe to every force that opposes him: *Enough!*

Martin Luther read this psalm and wrote one of the most famous hymns in Christian history: "A Mighty Fortress Is Our God." He understood that the fortress isn't a building. It's a person.

Psalm 46 is deeply personal to me. I have recited it more times than I can count, including during the worst season of my life, when my son died. When the earth beneath me was giving way, these words held me together. They didn't make the pain disappear. But they reminded me that the God who cannot be shaken was standing in the middle of it with me.

PSALM 91: SHELTER AND SHADOW

Psalm 91 piles up protection imagery like a fortress being built brick by brick. "Whoever dwells in the shelter of the Most High will rest in the shadow of the Almighty. I will say of the LORD, 'He is my refuge and my fortress, my God, in whom I trust.'"

Shelter. Shadow. Refuge. Fortress. Four images in two verses, all saying the same thing: God is the safest place you can be.

The psalm goes further. God will cover you "with his feathers, and under his wings you will find refuge." The image is of a mother bird spreading her wings over her young, shielding them from danger with her own body. God's protection is personal, intimate, and physical. He doesn't just command safety from a distance. He covers you.

Then comes a sweeping promise: "A thousand may fall at your side, ten thousand at your right hand, but it will not come near you." Arrows flying in the day. Pestilence stalking in the darkness. Terror at night. None of it will touch you. Angels will guard you. You will trample lions and cobras.

It's a staggering psalm. And it's the one Satan quoted.

When Jesus was being tempted in the wilderness (Matthew 4:5–7), the devil took him to the highest point of the temple and said, "If you are the Son of God, throw yourself down. For it is written: 'He will command his angels concerning you, and they will lift you up in their hands, so that you will not strike your foot against a stone.'"

Satan was quoting Psalm 91. And he was using it to twist trust into recklessness. The psalm promises God's protection, but it doesn't promise that we can manufacture dangerous situations and force God to bail us out. Jesus saw through it immediately. "It is also written," he replied, "'Do not put the Lord your God to the test.'"

This is one of the most important lessons in the entire Psalms. Trust in God is not the same thing as testing God. Real confidence doesn't throw itself off a cliff to see what happens. It walks through the valley because that's where the path leads, and it trusts the Shepherd to be there.

WHAT THIS MEANS FOR US

First, courage isn't the absence of fear. It's trust in the presence of fear. Every psalm in this chapter was written by someone who was afraid. What made them different wasn't that they didn't feel the danger. It was that they knew someone bigger than the danger.

Second, God's presence doesn't remove the valley. It walks through it with you. Psalm 23 doesn't promise a life without dark valleys. It promises a shepherd who won't leave you alone in them. The path still goes through. But you're not walking it by yourself.

Third, the safest place you can be is with God. Not safe as in nothing bad will ever happen. Safe as in the deepest part of who you are is held by someone who cannot be shaken, even when everything around you is falling apart. Mountains crumble. God doesn't.

Fourth, trust can be twisted. Satan used Psalm 91 to tempt Jesus, and the same move still works today. People take promises about God's protection and turn them into reasons to be reckless or presumptuous. Real, biblical trust doesn't demand that God prove himself. It rests in what he's already shown.

TALKING POINTS

1. **Psalm 23 says the shepherd leads through the valley, not around it.** Why do you think God doesn't always remove us from hard situations? What can we learn by going through difficulty instead of being spared from it?

2. **Psalm 46 says "Be still, and know that I am God." In context, this is a command to the nations to stop fighting.** How does that change the way you understand that verse? What does it mean to "be still" when life is chaotic?

3. **Psalm 91 uses the image of God covering his people with his wings.** What does that picture communicate about God's protection that a word like "fortress" doesn't? Why do you think the Bible uses so many different images for the same idea?

4. **Satan quoted Psalm 91 to tempt Jesus.** What's the difference between trusting God and testing God? How can we tell the difference in our own lives?

5. **All three of these psalms were written by people who were genuinely afraid.** How does knowing that the psalmists were scared change the way you read their words of trust? Is it encouraging to know that faith and fear can exist at the same time?

The trust psalms are songs for people who are standing in the dark, looking for solid ground. They don't promise that the dark will disappear. They promise something better: that the God who made the ground beneath your feet is standing on it with you.

But sometimes the darkness isn't just around you. It's in you. Sometimes the thing you need to bring to God isn't fear. It's guilt. The next psalms are for those moments, the ones where the hardest truth you have to face is what you've done.

Turn the page.

7

WHEN YOU'RE SORRY

Have you ever done something wrong and tried to keep it hidden? Not a small thing. Something that sat in your stomach like a rock. Something you thought about when you woke up and again before you fell asleep. Maybe you lied to someone who trusted you. Maybe you said something cruel that you couldn't take back. Maybe you got away with it, and nobody found out, but that almost made it worse, because now you had to carry it alone.

You know what that weight feels like. The way it follows you around. The way it makes it hard to look certain people in the eye. The way you start building walls around the secret, and the walls take more energy to maintain than the original mistake ever cost.

The Bible has a word for what happens when you finally stop hiding and tell the truth. It's called confession. And two psalms in particular describe what it feels like to carry the weight of hidden sin, and what it feels like to finally set it down.

TWO CONFESSIONS

Both Psalm 32 and Psalm 51 are connected to David, the king of Israel, and tradition links them to the worst chapter of his life.

Here's what happened. David, the man the Bible calls "a man after God's own heart," committed adultery with a woman named Bathsheba. When she became pregnant, David tried to cover it up. When the cover-up failed, he arranged for her husband, Uriah, to be killed in battle. It worked. Nobody knew. David married Bathsheba, and from the outside, everything looked fine.

But God knew. He sent the prophet Nathan to confront David with a story about a rich man who stole a poor man's only lamb. David was furious at the injustice. "The man who did this deserves to die!" he declared. And Nathan looked him in the eye and said four words that shattered everything: "You are the man."

Psalm 51 is the prayer David wrote after that confrontation. Psalm 32 is the song he wrote after God forgave him. Together, they form the most honest picture of sin, confession, and forgiveness in the entire Bible.

PSALM 32: THE WEIGHT OF SILENCE

Psalm 32 doesn't start with the confession. It starts with the relief that comes after. "Blessed is the one whose transgressions are forgiven, whose sins are covered. Blessed is the one whose sin the Lord does not count against them."

The psalmist knows what forgiveness feels like because he knows what unforgiveness felt like. And in verses 3–4, he describes the cost of keeping his sin hidden: "When I kept silent, my bones wasted away through my groaning all day long. For day and night your hand was heavy on me; my strength was sapped as in the heat of summer."

This isn't just guilt as an emotion. It's guilt as a physical experience. His body was breaking down. He felt drained, heavy, exhausted. The silence wasn't protecting him. It was destroying him. He was carrying something he was never meant to carry, and it was crushing him from the inside out.

Then comes verse 5, and everything changes in a single sentence: "Then I acknowledged my sin to you and did not cover up my iniquity. I said, 'I will confess my transgressions to the LORD,' and you forgave the guilt of my sin."

Notice how fast the forgiveness comes. There's no waiting period. No probation. No list of conditions. He confessed, and God forgave. The weight he had been carrying for who knows how long was gone in one honest moment.

The rest of the psalm flows from that relief. The psalmist urges everyone who belongs to God to pray honestly when they sin. He describes God as a hiding place, a protector, someone who surrounds him with "songs of deliverance." And then he turns teacher, urging others not to be stubborn like a horse or mule that has to be dragged with a bit and bridle. Don't wait, he's saying. Don't make God drag the confession out of you. Come willingly. Come quickly. The freedom on the other side is worth it.

PSALM 51: CREATE IN ME A CLEAN HEART

Psalm 32 describes the before and after. Psalm 51 takes you inside the confession itself.

The opening is a plea: "Have mercy on me, O God, according to your unfailing love; according to your great compassion blot out my transgressions. Wash away all my iniquity and cleanse me from my sin."

Three requests in two verses: blot out, wash, cleanse. The psalmist isn't asking once and moving on. He's piling up the requests because the sin feels that deep. He needs it removed, scrubbed, erased. He's covered in it and he knows it.

Then comes an admission that cuts to the bone: "Against you, you only, have I sinned and done what is evil in your sight." Given what David did, this might seem strange. He sinned against Bathsheba. He sinned against Uriah. He sinned against his own family. But the psalmist isn't saying those people don't matter. He's saying that every sin, no matter who it hurts, is ultimately an offense against God. The human consequences are devastating, but the deepest wound is the one between the sinner and the God who made him.

The psalm goes further than most people expect. The psalmist doesn't just ask for forgiveness. He asks to be remade: "Create in me a pure heart, O God, and renew a steadfast spirit within me."

That word "create" is the same word used in Genesis 1 when God made the heavens and the earth. The psalmist isn't asking for a minor adjustment. He's asking for something only God can do: to reach inside him and build something new where the old thing rotted. He knows that forgiveness alone isn't enough. He needs to be different, or he'll end up right back where he started.

And then comes the line that reveals his deepest fear: "Do not cast me from your presence or take your Holy Spirit from me."

The worst consequence of sin, for the psalmist, isn't punishment. It's separation from God. He would rather endure anything than lose the presence of God in his life. That's what real repentance looks like. It's not just wanting the consequences to go away. It's wanting God back.

The psalm closes with a statement that shocked the original audience: "You do not delight in sacrifice, or I would bring it; you do not take pleasure in burnt offerings. My sacrifice, O God, is a broken spirit; a broken and contrite heart you, O God, will not despise."

In a culture built around animal sacrifice, this was radical. God isn't impressed by rituals performed with a hard heart. What he wants is honesty. Brokenness. A heart that knows it failed and isn't trying to spin it. You can bring a thousand bulls to the altar, but if your heart isn't broken over what you've done, God isn't interested. Bring the brokenness instead. That's the offering he accepts.

REGRET AND REPENTANCE

These two psalms reveal something important about the difference between regret and repentance.

Regret says, "I feel bad about what happened." Repentance says, "I did this, it was wrong, and I'm turning around."

Regret focuses on consequences. *I wish I hadn't gotten caught. I wish this didn't hurt so much. I wish things could go back to how they were.* Repentance focuses on the offense itself. *I sinned against God. I need to be forgiven. I need to change.*

Saul, Israel's first king, showed regret when the prophet Samuel confronted him. He said the right words, but his real concern was how things looked in front of the people. David showed repentance. He didn't make excuses. He didn't blame anyone else. He owned what he did, asked God for mercy, and begged to be transformed.

That's the difference between Saul and David, and it's the difference between these psalms and a hollow apology. Real confession doesn't spin. It doesn't manage the fallout. It falls on its face before God and says, "I have nothing to offer except the truth. Please don't let it be too late."

WHAT THIS MEANS FOR US

First, hidden sin will eat you alive. Psalm 32 is as honest about the cost of silence as it is about the relief of confession. Keeping secrets doesn't protect you. It drains you. The energy it takes to hide what you've done will always cost more than the honesty you're avoiding.

Second, God already knows. You're not confessing to inform God. He knew before you did it. Confession isn't about giving God new information. It's about agreeing with what he already sees and choosing honesty over pretense.

Third, forgiveness is available right now. Psalm 32 shows forgiveness arriving the moment confession happens. You don't have to earn your way back. You don't have to serve a sentence first. God's unfailing love is the basis for forgiveness, not your performance.

Fourth, real repentance asks for transformation, not just relief. Psalm 51 goes beyond "forgive me" to "change me." If all you want is for the guilt to stop, that's regret. If you want to be a different person, that's repentance. And God responds to repentance with new creation.

Fifth, a broken heart is the offering God wants. Not perfection. Not impressive religious performance. Brokenness. Honesty. The willingness to stand before God with nothing in your hands and say, "This is who I am, and I need you."

TALKING POINTS

1. **Psalm 32 describes the physical effects of unconfessed sin: wasted bones, constant groaning, drained strength.** Have you ever noticed that guilt affects you physically, not just emotionally? Why do you think that happens?

2. **David says in Psalm 51, "Against you, you only, have I sinned."** What does he mean by that, given that his sin clearly hurt other people? Why is the offense against God the deepest part of sin?

3. **The psalmist in Psalm 51 asks God to "create" a clean heart in him, using the same word from Genesis 1.** What does it mean that only God can create something truly new in us? Why can't we just fix ourselves?

4. **This chapter draws a distinction between regret and repentance.** What's the difference between regret and repentance? Can you think of examples from your own life or from stories you know where someone showed one but not the other?

5. **Psalm 51 says God doesn't want sacrifices performed with a hard heart. He wants "a broken and contrite heart."** Why do you think brokenness matters more to God than religious performance? What does that tell us about what God values?

These are the hardest psalms to pray, because they require something most of us resist with everything we have: total honesty about who we are and what we've done. But they're also the most freeing psalms in the book, because on the other side of that honesty is a God who doesn't turn away from broken people. He makes them new.

There's another kind of honesty in the Psalms, though, and it's even more uncomfortable. It's the psalms where the writer isn't confessing sin. He's expressing rage. Not at himself, but at the people who hurt him. And the things he asks God to do to those people will shock you.

Turn the page.

8

WHEN YOU'RE ANGRY

Few characters in literature are more hateful than Mr. Murdstone. Early in Charles Dickens' *David Copperfield*, young David's life changes overnight when his gentle mother marries this cold, controlling man. Murdstone and his equally cruel sister take over the household. They humiliate David. They beat him. They crush his mother's spirit until she's a shadow of who she used to be. When she dies, broken and exhausted, the Murdstones don't grieve. They send David to work in a factory. He's a child, and nobody protects him.

If you've read those chapters, you know the feeling. It's not sadness. It's something hotter. It's the desire for someone to step in and make things right. You want someone to look at the Murdstones and say, "Enough. You will not get away with this." You want justice, and you want it now.

That feeling is all over the Bible. And the Psalms don't just acknowledge it. They give it a voice.

THE PSALMS MOST PEOPLE SKIP

Every type of psalm we've looked at so far gets taught in churches and printed on bookmarks. Praise psalms, trust psalms, thanksgiving psalms, even laments sometimes show up in Sunday school. But there's a category of psalms that most people quietly skip over, and when they do encounter them, they don't know what to do.

They're called imprecatory psalms, and they're the prayers where the psalmist asks God to punish, destroy, or curse his enemies. Not gently. Not with a slap on the wrist. These psalms ask God to break teeth, pour out wrath, and wipe the wicked off the face of the earth.

If that sounds shocking, it should. These are some of the most uncomfortable passages in the Bible. But they're there for a reason, and pretending they don't exist doesn't help anyone. The Bible included them because God knows that his people sometimes feel a rage so deep that the only safe place to put it is in his hands.

PSALM 58: BREAK THEIR TEETH

Psalm 58 is aimed at rulers who have power and use it to destroy the innocent. The psalmist looks at a world run by corrupt leaders and asks a blunt question: "Do you rulers indeed speak justly? Do you judge people with equity?" The answer, obviously, is no. These leaders deal out violence and injustice as casually as dealing cards.

The psalmist compares them to a cobra that can't be charmed, deaf to any appeal, dangerous no matter what. These aren't people who made a mistake. These are people who have chosen cruelty as a way of life.

And then the psalmist turns to God and lets loose: "Break the teeth in their mouths, O God; LORD, tear out the fangs of those lions! Let them vanish like water that flows away; when they draw the bow, let their arrows fall short. Like a slug that melts away as it moves along, like a stillborn child that never sees the sun."

Break their teeth. Let them dissolve like slugs. Let them be stillborn. This isn't polite language. This isn't a measured request for mild correction. This is someone who has watched the powerful crush the weak and is absolutely furious about it.

The psalm ends with the righteous rejoicing when justice finally comes, a scene so graphic it makes modern readers flinch: "The righteous will be glad when they are avenged, when they dip their feet in the blood of the wicked."

You might be thinking, *How is this in the Bible?* Hold that thought. We'll come back to it.

PSALM 137: BEAUTY AND BRUTALITY

Psalm 137 might be the most emotionally complex poem in the entire book. It starts with one of the most beautiful and heartbreaking images in Scripture, and it ends with one of the most horrifying.

The setting is Babylon. The Israelites have been conquered and dragged into exile. Their city is destroyed. Their temple is gone. Everything they knew and loved has been ripped away. And now they're sitting by the rivers of Babylon, weeping, their harps hanging silent in the trees.

"By the rivers of Babylon we sat and wept when we remembered Zion. There on the poplars we hung our harps, for there our captors asked us for songs, our tormentors demanded songs of joy; they said, 'Sing us one of the songs of Zion!'"

Their captors are taunting them. "Sing us one of your songs!" It's not a sincere request. It's mockery. It's the ancient equivalent of a bully making you dance after he's already knocked you down. The captors want entertainment from the very people they've destroyed.

The response is one of the most passionate vows in the Bible: "How can we sing the songs of the LORD while in a foreign land? If I forget you, Jerusalem, may my right hand forget its skill. May my tongue cling to the roof of my mouth if I do not remember you, if I do not consider Jerusalem my highest joy."

Up to this point, the psalm is devastating but beautiful. It's about grief, loyalty, and the refusal to let captivity erase what matters most. If the psalm stopped here, it would be one of the most beloved passages in the Bible.

But it doesn't stop.

"Daughter Babylon, doomed to destruction, happy is the one who repays you according to what you have done to us. Happy is the one who seizes your infants and dashes them against the rocks."

There it is. The verse that makes people close their Bibles.

The psalmist is asking God to do to Babylon what Babylon did to Israel. When the Babylonian army destroyed Jerusalem, they didn't spare the children. The psalmist has seen things no person should ever have to see, and his rage is so enormous that the only way he can express it is by praying the most terrible prayer in the book.

HANDING YOUR ANGER TO GOD

So what do we do with these psalms? Are they the sinful outbursts of angry people that should be removed from our Bibles? Should we pretend they aren't there?

No. And here's why.

The imprecatory psalms aren't just explosions of rage. They're prayers. They're directed at God. And that makes all the difference.

Think about what the psalmist is *not* doing. He's not picking up a sword and going after his enemies himself. He's not forming an army. He's not plotting revenge. He's bringing his fury to God and saying, "You deal with this. I'm trusting you to make it right."

That's actually the opposite of taking matters into your own hands. It's the ultimate act of surrender. The psalmist is so angry he can barely see straight, but instead of acting on that anger, he places it in God's hands and says, "I trust you to be the judge. Not me. You."

The New Testament makes this same point directly. Paul writes: "Do not take revenge, my dear friends, but leave room for God's wrath, for it is written: 'It is mine to avenge; I will repay,' says the Lord" (Romans 12:19). Don't take revenge. Leave room for God. Hand the anger over.

That's exactly what the imprecatory psalms do. They hand the anger to God, honestly and completely, and they let him decide what to do with it. They don't pretend the rage doesn't exist. They don't bury it under polite language. They bring the full, ugly truth to God because he's the only one who can carry it.

And that's actually safer than the alternative. Anger that gets buried doesn't go away. It festers. It comes out sideways, in bitterness, cruelty, or despair. The psalmists understood that the only safe place for rage at injustice is before the throne of a just God. Better to scream it at him than to let it poison you from the inside.

WHAT THIS MEANS FOR US

First, anger at injustice is not a sin. When you see someone being bullied, exploited, or crushed by someone more powerful, the anger you feel is appropriate. God himself is angry at injustice. The problem isn't the anger. It's what you do with it.

Second, what you do with anger matters more than what you feel. The psalmists felt murderous rage. But they didn't act on it. They prayed it. They handed it to God. There's a world of difference between wanting revenge and asking God to bring justice. One puts you in the judge's seat. The other puts God there.

Third, God doesn't need you to sanitize your prayers. If you're furious, say so. If you want God to stop someone who's hurting people, tell him. He already knows what you're thinking. Pretending you're not angry doesn't fool God. It just keeps you from being honest with the only one who can actually do something about it.

Fourth, these psalms don't give you permission to hate. They give you permission to be honest about your pain and then release it. The goal of praying an imprecation isn't to stay angry forever. It's to give the anger to God so it stops controlling you. You name it, you hand it over, and you trust him to act justly, even if his justice looks different from what you imagined.

TALKING POINTS

1. **Psalm 58 describes corrupt rulers who use their power to harm the innocent.** Can you think of situations today where people in power abuse those beneath them? Why do you think injustice makes us so angry?

2. **Psalm 137 begins with some of the most beautiful lines in the Bible and ends with some of the most disturbing.** How do you hold both together? Does knowing the backstory of what Babylon did to Israel change the way you read the ending?

3. **The imprecatory psalms direct anger at God rather than acting on it personally.** What's the difference between praying for God to bring justice and taking revenge yourself? Why does it matter where you aim your anger?

4. **Paul tells Christians not to take revenge but to "leave room for God's wrath" (Romans 12:19).** How does this connect to the imprecatory psalms? Is it possible to forgive someone and still want God to bring justice?

5. **Some people think the angry psalms should be removed from the Bible. Others think they're essential.** What do you think? Why might it be important for the Bible to include prayers this raw and uncomfortable?

The imprecatory psalms are the hardest songs in the book. They force us to look at what human beings are capable of doing to each other, and they refuse to let us pretend the Bible is always gentle and comfortable. But they also point to a God who takes injustice seriously, who invites us to bring our worst feelings to him, and who promises that one day, every wrong will be made right.

The Psalms have shown us praise, pain, trust, gratitude, guilt, and rage. But there are still psalms that don't fit neatly into any of those categories. They're the quiet ones, the ones that sit down and think about what it means to live well. They ask the question every generation asks: How should I live?

Turn the page.

9

WHEN YOU'RE TRYING TO DO THE RIGHT THING

At the beginning of *The Super Mario Bros. Movie*, Mario isn't winning. His plumbing business is struggling. People mock him. A commercial he and Luigi made becomes a public joke. Nobody takes him seriously. Meanwhile, Bowser has everything: a massive army, unstoppable power, an entire kingdom under his control. He rolls through the Mushroom Kingdom crushing anyone in his path, and nobody seems able to stop him.

If you paused the movie right there and asked who's going to come out on top, you'd pick Bowser every time. He has the power. He has the resources. He has the intimidation. Mario is a short plumber from Brooklyn who can barely catch a break.

But you know how the story ends. The guy who looked like a loser kept showing up, kept fighting, kept choosing courage over fear. And the guy who had all the power lost everything.

The Psalms have a whole category of songs about exactly this tension. The righteous seem to struggle. The wicked seem to win. And the question hanging over everything is: *Does doing the right thing actually matter?*

THE THINKING PSALMS

Wisdom psalms are different from anything else we've looked at. They're not prayers or worship songs in the traditional sense. They're more like meditations, poems where the writer sits down and thinks hard about how life works. What makes a good life? Why do bad people sometimes prosper? Is there a pattern to the universe, and if so, what is it?

These psalms share their DNA with books like Proverbs, Job, and Ecclesiastes, the Bible's wisdom literature. They use the same vocabulary: the righteous and the wicked, the wise and the foolish, the path of life and the path of destruction. And they wrestle with the same question those books wrestle with: Does obedience to God actually lead somewhere good?

Three wisdom psalms tackle this question from three different angles, and together they form one of the clearest pictures of how the Bible thinks about right and wrong.

PSALM 1: TWO PATHS

Psalm 1 is the front door of the entire book of Psalms. It was placed first on purpose. Before you read a single praise song or lament or prayer, the editors want you to stand in front of this psalm and make a choice.

The psalm describes two kinds of people. The first is the one who "does not walk in step with the wicked or stand in the way that sinners take or sit in the company of mockers, but whose delight is in the law of the LORD, and who meditates on his law day and night."

Notice the progression: walk, stand, sit. Each step represents a deeper involvement with the wrong crowd. You start by walking past. Then you stop and stand with them. Then you sit down and make yourself at home. Sin isn't usually a sudden leap. It's a slow drift, and the psalm wants you to see the drift before it carries you away.

The person who avoids that drift and instead delights in God's Word is compared to "a tree planted by streams of water, which yields its fruit in season and whose leaf does not wither. Whatever they do prospers."

A tree. Rooted. Alive. Producing fruit. Fed by a constant source of water. That's the image of a life built on God's instruction.

The wicked get a very different image: "They are like chaff that the wind blows away." Chaff is the dry, useless husk that separates from the grain during harvest. It has no roots, no weight, no value. The wind picks it up and it's gone.

Two paths. Two destinations. One leads to life and rootedness. The other leads to nothing. Psalm 1 puts you at the crossroads and says: choose.

PSALM 37: DON'T ENVY THE WICKED

Psalm 1 makes the two paths sound clean and simple. Psalm 37 acknowledges that it doesn't always feel that way. The psalm opens with a command that immediately tells you someone is struggling: "Do not fret because of those who are evil or be envious of those who do wrong."

You don't tell someone not to fret unless they're already fretting. And you don't warn against envy unless it's already gnawing at them. The psalmist is speaking to people who are watching the wicked prosper and thinking, *Why am I even trying?*

The answer comes in layers. First, the success of the wicked is temporary: "For like the grass they will soon wither, like green plants they will soon die away." They look alive now, but they have no root system. Give it time.

Second, trust God and keep doing good: "Trust in the LORD and do good; dwell in the land and enjoy safe pasture. Take delight in the LORD, and he will give you the desires of your heart."

Third, and this is the hardest part, be patient: "Be still before the LORD and wait patiently for him; do not fret when people succeed in their ways, when they carry out their wicked schemes."

Wait patiently. That's hard advice when the person cutting corners at school gets the better grade, or the kid who bullies everyone seems to have all the friends, or the people who cheat in life seem to keep winning. Psalm 37 doesn't deny that this happens. It just says: *don't let it change who you are.*

The psalm circles back to the same point again and again: "I was young and now I am old, yet I have never seen the righteous forsaken or their children begging bread." The psalmist has lived long enough to see the full picture, and what he's seen is that the wicked don't last, even when they look invincible.

Jesus quoted this psalm directly. In the Sermon on the Mount, he said, "Blessed are the meek, for they will inherit the earth" (Matthew 5:5), echoing Psalm 37:11: "The meek will inherit the land and enjoy peace and prosperity." The people who look like losers now are the ones who end up with everything.

PSALM 73: ALMOST LOSING FAITH

Psalm 73 is the most honest of the three, because the psalmist doesn't just acknowledge the problem. He admits he almost quit.

The psalm was written by a man named Asaph, a worship leader in the temple. He opens with a conclusion he barely held onto: "Surely God is good to Israel, to those who are pure in heart."

Then he admits how close he came to losing that conviction: "But as for me, my feet had almost slipped; I had nearly lost my foothold. For I envied the arrogant when I saw the prosperity of the wicked."

What follows is one of the most painfully honest passages in the Bible. Asaph describes everything the wicked have: healthy bodies, no struggles, freedom from the burdens other people carry. They're proud, violent, and mocking, and they get away with all of it. "They have no struggles; their bodies are healthy and strong. They are free from common human burdens."

And then Asaph voices the thought that was eating him alive: "Surely in vain I have kept my heart pure and have washed my hands in innocence. All day long I have been afflicted, and every morning brings new punishments."

What's the point of being good if this is what I get? He followed God's rules. He kept his heart clean. And all he got was pain, while the people who ignored God got everything he wanted.

This is the most dangerous moment in the psalm, and Asaph knows it. He says, "If I had spoken out like that, I would have betrayed your children." He held his tongue because he didn't want to destroy someone else's faith with his doubts. But holding it in was "oppressive" to him. He was stuck.

Then came the turning point: "Till I entered the sanctuary of God; then I understood their final destiny."

Something happened when Asaph went to worship. The text doesn't explain what he saw or heard. Maybe it was the reminder of God's holiness. Maybe it was the weight of God's presence after weeks of running on his own reasoning. Whatever it was, it recalibrated his entire perspective. He suddenly saw the wicked not as winners but as people standing on slippery ground, headed for destruction. Their prosperity was a dream they hadn't woken up from yet.

And then Asaph turned the lens on himself: "When my heart was grieved and my spirit embittered, I was senseless and ignorant; I was a brute beast before you."

He's not gentle with himself. He calls his own envy what it was: ignorant, senseless, beastly. But then comes one of the most beautiful lines in the Psalms: "Yet I am always with you; you hold me by my right hand. You guide me with your counsel, and afterward you will take me into glory."

Even when Asaph was at his worst, God never let go of his hand. That's the answer. Not an explanation for why the wicked prosper. Not a formula for when justice will arrive. Just this: God is with you, and he's not letting go, and the end of the story hasn't been written yet.

WHAT THIS MEANS FOR US

First, the right path doesn't always feel like the winning path. Psalm 1 makes the choice clear, but Psalms 37 and 73 admit that living on the right path often feels like losing. The

Bible doesn't pretend that doing the right thing always pays off immediately. It insists that it pays off ultimately.

Second, envy is more dangerous than you think. Asaph nearly lost his faith because he couldn't stop comparing his life to the lives of the wicked. Comparison will wreck you faster than almost anything else. Guard your eyes.

Third, when your thinking gets clouded, go to God. Asaph didn't figure things out by reasoning harder. He went to the sanctuary. He put himself in God's presence. Sometimes the answer to a faith crisis isn't a better argument. It's worship.

Fourth, God holds your hand even when you're slipping. Asaph was bitter, envious, and calling himself a beast, and God was still holding on. You don't lose God's grip by having doubts. You lose it by walking away. And even then, he's reaching for you.

TALKING POINTS

1. **Psalm 1 describes the righteous person as a tree and the wicked as chaff.** What makes those two images so effective? Which one would you rather be, and what would it take to live like the tree?

2. **Psalm 37 says "do not fret" three times.** Why is it so hard not to be bothered when people who cheat or lie seem to get ahead? How do you keep doing the right thing when it doesn't seem to matter?

3. **Asaph almost lost his faith because the wicked seemed to have everything.** Have you ever felt that way? What pulled you back?

4. **The turning point in Psalm 73 came when Asaph "entered the sanctuary of God."** What do you think happened

there? Why does being in God's presence change the way we see things?

5. **Asaph says God was holding his hand even when he was at his most bitter and confused.** What does that tell you about how God treats people who are struggling with doubt?

The wisdom psalms ask the hardest question of all: Is it worth it? Is doing the right thing, following God, choosing integrity over shortcuts, actually worth the cost? The answer is yes, but the Psalms are honest enough to admit that the "yes" sometimes takes a lifetime to see.

There's one more group of psalms that also looks ahead, but not just to the end of a life. These psalms look ahead to the end of the story itself, to a king who was coming, one greater than David, greater than Solomon, greater than anyone the world had ever seen.

Turn the page.

10

WHEN YOU'RE WAITING FOR A KING

Mark Twain's *The Prince and the Pauper* tells the story of two boys in sixteenth-century England who look exactly alike. One is Prince Edward, heir to the throne. The other is Tom Canty, a beggar's son from the London slums. When they accidentally switch places, nobody notices. The prince walks into the streets dressed in rags, and everyone treats him like trash. The pauper sits on the throne dressed in silk, and everyone bows.

The whole story runs on a single unsettling idea: people look at the clothes, not the person. The real king is out there, but nobody recognizes him because he doesn't look the part.

The Psalms contain a group of songs that were written for Israel's kings, songs about coronations and battles and thrones. But as centuries passed and the kings kept failing, these psalms started pointing beyond any earthly ruler toward a king who hadn't come yet. And when he finally arrived, he looked nothing like what anyone expected. He wasn't wearing a crown. He was wearing a carpenter's apron.

SONGS FOR A THRONE

Royal psalms are psalms that focus on the king, either as the subject or the speaker. Some were written for coronation ceremonies. Some were prayers asking God to bless the king with justice and victory. Some were pre-battle songs declaring that God would fight on the king's behalf.

During the time of David and his descendants, these psalms had an immediate, practical purpose. A new king took the throne, and the nation sang Psalm 2. The army prepared for battle, and they sang Psalm 110. The people prayed for their ruler's reign, and they sang Psalm 72.

But here's the problem. The kings kept disappointing. David was great, but he sinned terribly. Solomon started well, but ended as an oppressor. After Solomon, the kingdom split in two, and most of the kings who followed were disasters. The monarchy eventually collapsed when Babylon destroyed Jerusalem in 586 BC and carried the people into exile. The throne was empty.

So what were faithful Israelites supposed to do with psalms that promised an unshakable king, a worldwide reign, and enemies crushed under the king's feet? The kings were gone. The throne was dust.

They started reading these psalms differently. Instead of looking backward at the kings they had, they started looking forward to a king they were still waiting for. A future anointed one. A Messiah. Someone who would finally be everything these psalms described.

PSALM 2: THE NATIONS RAGE

Psalm 2 opens with a scene of global rebellion: "Why do the nations conspire and the peoples plot in vain? The kings of the earth rise up and the rulers band together, against the LORD and against his anointed."

The world's most powerful people are conspiring against God and his chosen king. They want to break free from God's authority, throw off his rule, and run things their own way.

God's response? He laughs. "The One enthroned in heaven laughs; the Lord scoffs at them." This isn't the warm laughter of amusement. This is the laughter of someone who sees a toddler trying to push over a mountain. The nations think they're powerful. God knows they're nothing.

Then God speaks, and his words are terrifying: "I have installed my king on Zion, my holy mountain." No matter what the nations do, God's king is already on the throne. Their rebellion changes nothing.

The psalm then records God's decree to the king: "You are my son; today I have become your father. Ask me, and I will make the nations your inheritance, the ends of the earth your possession."

In its original setting, this was spoken at the coronation of a new Davidic king. God was declaring a special father-son relationship with the ruler. But no Israelite king ever received "the nations" as his inheritance. No Davidic king ever ruled "the ends of the earth." The psalm was always bigger than the person wearing the crown.

When Jesus was baptized, a voice from heaven said, "You are my Son, whom I love; with you I am well pleased" (Mark

1:11), echoing Psalm 2:7 directly. The early church recognized that Herod, Pilate, and the religious leaders who conspired against Jesus were the raging nations of Psalm 2 (Acts 4:25–26). And the book of Revelation pictures Jesus returning with an iron scepter to rule the nations (Revelation 19:15), fulfilling the promise of Psalm 2:9.

The psalm that was too big for any earthly king fit Jesus perfectly.

PSALM 72: THE KING NOBODY COULD BE

Psalm 72 is a prayer for the king, and the requests are staggering. "Endow the king with your justice, O God, the royal son with your righteousness. May he judge your people in righteousness, your afflicted ones with justice."

The prayer asks for a king who rules with perfect fairness, who defends the oppressed, who rescues the needy. "For he will deliver the needy who cry out, the afflicted who have no one to help. He will take pity on the weak and the needy and save the needy from death."

But it doesn't stop there. The psalm also prays that this king's reign would extend across the entire earth: "May he rule from sea to sea and from the River to the ends of the earth. May all kings bow down to him and all nations serve him."

And then: "May his name endure forever; may it continue as long as the sun. Then all nations will be blessed through him, and they will call him blessed."

That last line is a direct echo of God's promise to Abraham in Genesis 12:3, that through his descendants all the nations of the earth would be blessed. The psalmist is praying for a king who would fulfill the oldest promise in Israel's story.

No king ever did. Solomon came closest, but even he became an oppressor who burdened his own people. Every Davidic king fell short of this prayer. The prayer itself became a kind of prophecy, a description of a king so just, so compassionate, so powerful, and so universal that only God himself could fill the role.

When wise men from eastern nations traveled to Bethlehem carrying gold for a newborn king (Matthew 2:1–11), the early church saw Psalm 72:10–11 coming true: "May the kings of Tarshish and of distant shores bring tribute to him. May the kings of Sheba and Seba present him gifts."

The prayer for the king nobody could be was answered by a baby in a manger.

PSALM 110: THE MOST QUOTED PSALM

Psalm 110 holds a unique distinction: the New Testament quotes or references it more than any other psalm. Jesus himself used it in an argument with the religious leaders, and the author of Hebrews built an entire theological argument on top of it.

The psalm opens with a divine oracle: "The LORD says to my lord: 'Sit at my right hand until I make your enemies a footstool for your feet.'"

God is speaking to the king and telling him to sit in the place of highest honor while God himself defeats the king's enemies. The king doesn't have to fight alone. God will crush the opposition and place it under the king's feet.

Then comes the surprise. Verse 4 introduces a second oracle: "The LORD has sworn and will not change his mind: 'You are a priest forever, in the order of Melchizedek.'"

In Israel, kings and priests were separate roles. Kings ruled. Priests served in the temple. Mixing the two was forbidden. When King Saul tried to perform a priestly duty, it cost him his kingdom (1 Samuel 13). But Psalm 110 says this king will also be a priest, not in the line of Aaron, the first high priest, but in the line of Melchizedek, a mysterious priest-king who appeared briefly in Genesis 14 and then vanished from the story.

This combination of king and priest in one person didn't fit any ruler in Israel's history. It was a puzzle waiting for a solution.

Jesus provided it. He used Psalm 110 to argue that the Messiah was greater than David, not just his descendant (Matthew 22:41–46). After his resurrection, the early church declared that Jesus had "sat down at the right hand of God" (Acts 2:34–35), fulfilling the first oracle. And the author of Hebrews spent multiple chapters explaining how Jesus is the ultimate high priest "in the order of Melchizedek" (Hebrews 5–7), fulfilling the second.

King and priest. Ruler and mediator. The one who reigns over everything and the one who stands between God and his people. No one in the Old Testament could be both. Jesus is both.

WHAT THIS MEANS FOR US

First, the psalms were always pointing to someone bigger. The royal psalms described a king no human could fully be.

That wasn't a failure. It was a promise. Every gap between what the psalms described and what the kings delivered was an arrow pointing forward to Jesus.

Second, Jesus is the king the world is still raging against. Psalm 2 isn't ancient history. The pattern of nations and leaders conspiring against God's authority is as current as today's headlines. But God's response hasn't changed either. He still laughs at his opponents with derision. His king is still on the throne, and no rebellion will unseat him.

Third, Jesus is both king and priest. He has the authority to rule and the compassion to intercede. He doesn't just sit on a throne giving orders. He stands between you and God, representing you, advocating for you, offering himself on your behalf. No other king has ever done that.

Fourth, the promises aren't finished yet. The royal psalms look forward to a day when every knee bows and every nation is blessed through God's king. That hasn't fully happened yet. But it will. The same psalms that predicted Jesus' first coming also predict his return, and everything they describe will come true.

TALKING POINTS

1. **Psalm 2 says God laughs at the nations that rebel against him.** What does that tell you about how God views human power compared to his own? Is that comforting or unsettling to you?

2. **Psalm 72 describes a king who defends the poor, rules with justice, and blesses all nations.** Why do you think no human king ever lived up to this description? What does it mean that Jesus is the one who fulfills it?

3. Psalm 110 combines the roles of king and priest in one person. Why is it significant that Jesus is both? How does each role affect your relationship with him?

4. The royal psalms were written for real kings but ended up pointing to Jesus. Have you ever experienced something that turned out to mean more than you originally thought? How does that help you understand how God works through Scripture?

5. These psalms promise that one day every nation will acknowledge God's king. What do you think that will look like? How should that promise affect the way we live right now?

The royal psalms are the songs of a throne that was always waiting for the right king. For centuries, the chair sat empty or was occupied by someone who didn't quite fit. And then a carpenter's son from Nazareth walked into the story, and everything the psalms had been saying for a thousand years finally made sense.

But the Psalms aren't just about looking forward. Some of them are about looking around, at the people beside you on the road, the community walking toward God together. Those songs have their own beauty, and they're next.

Turn the page.

11

WHEN YOU'RE WALKING TOGETHER

Duchess and her three kittens are lost. Somewhere in the French countryside, miles from the warm Paris mansion they call home, they're stranded with no idea how to get back. That's the setup of Disney's *The Aristocats*, and if the story were only about getting from point A to point B, it would be a short film.

But along the way, they meet Thomas O'Malley, a street-wise alley cat who offers to guide them home. And then they meet his friends, a group of jazz-playing cats who throw the best party the kittens have ever seen. (I can neither affirm or deny that I used to dance to "Everybody Wants to be a Cat.")

The journey that started with fear and loneliness turns into something completely different. By the time they reach Paris, the trip has changed them. They've gained a family that's bigger than the one they started with.

The Psalms contain a set of fifteen songs that were written for a journey. They're called the Songs of Ascent (Psalms 120–134), and they were sung by Israelites making the trip to Jerusalem to worship at the temple during the great annual festivals. The destination mattered enormously. But so did the road, and so did the people walking it beside you.

SONGS FOR THE ROAD

Three times a year, faithful Israelites were expected to travel to Jerusalem for major festivals: Passover, Pentecost, and the Feast of Tabernacles. For many of them, this wasn't a quick trip. They lived in towns and villages scattered across the countryside, sometimes days away from the capital. The journey required planning, provisions, and courage, because the roads could be dangerous.

But they didn't go alone. Families joined together. Neighbors walked in groups. As they got closer to Jerusalem, the roads would have filled with more and more travelers, all heading the same direction, all singing the same songs. By the time they reached the hills surrounding the city, the crowd would have been enormous, a river of people flowing uphill toward the temple where God had made his presence known.

The Songs of Ascent were the soundtrack for that journey. Some were sung at the beginning, when home was far behind and the road ahead was uncertain. Some were sung as the travelers climbed the final hills and caught their first glimpse of Jerusalem's walls. Some were sung inside the temple courts, surrounded by thousands of fellow worshipers.

"Ascent" refers to the physical climb. Jerusalem sits on a ridge, so no matter which direction you approached from, the last stretch was uphill. But the word carried a spiritual meaning too. You weren't just climbing a hill. You were drawing closer to God.

Three of these pilgrim songs capture the heart of the collection.

PSALM 84: BETTER ONE DAY

Psalm 84 is the song of someone who can barely contain his excitement about getting to the temple. The opening line is pure longing: "How lovely is your dwelling place, LORD Almighty! My soul yearns, even faints, for the courts of the LORD; my heart and my flesh cry out for the living God."

This isn't casual interest. The psalmist's whole body aches for God's presence. He's so desperate to be in the temple that he envies the birds who've built nests near the altar. They get to live there. He only gets to visit.

The middle of the psalm describes the pilgrimage itself. "Blessed are those whose strength is in you, whose hearts are set on pilgrimage. As they pass through the Valley of Baka, they make it a place of springs; the autumn rains also cover it with pools. They go from strength to strength, till each appears before God in Zion."

The Valley of Baka means "the Valley of Weeping." It was apparently a dry, barren stretch on the road to Jerusalem. But the pilgrims transformed it. Their presence, their faith, their singing turned a weeping valley into a place of springs. And instead of growing weaker on the long road, they grew stronger. The closer they got to God, the more energy they had.

Then comes the line that captures everything: "Better is one day in your courts than a thousand elsewhere; I would rather be a doorkeeper in the house of my God than dwell in the tents of the wicked."

One day with God is worth more than a thousand days anywhere else. And the psalmist would rather have the lowest position in God's house, standing at the door, than the highest position among people who've turned away from God. Proximity to God is the only thing that matters.

PSALM 121: LOOKING TO THE HILLS

Psalm 121 is probably the most beloved of all the pilgrim songs, and it opens with a scene every traveler on the road to Jerusalem would have recognized. "I lift up my eyes to the mountains—where does my help come from? My help comes from the LORD, the Maker of heaven and earth."

The pilgrim looks up at the mountains surrounding Jerusalem. In Israel's history, the hills around Jerusalem were often filled with shrines to false gods. In the ancient world, mountains were associated with the divine, with the realm of the gods. But the psalmist isn't trusting in the mountains themselves. His help comes from the Lord who made them.

What follows is one of the most comforting passages in the Bible, built entirely on one idea: God watches over you. "He will not let your foot slip—he who watches over you will not slumber; indeed, he who watches over Israel will neither slumber nor sleep."

Other gods, the psalmist implies, might fall asleep on the job. The prophet Elijah once mocked the prophets of Baal for exactly that reason: "Maybe your god is sleeping and needs to be woken up" (1 Kings 18:27). But the Lord never sleeps. He is always watching, always guarding, always present.

"The LORD watches over you—the LORD is your shade

at your right hand; the sun will not harm you by day, nor the moon by night." For pilgrims walking through the hot, exposed terrain of ancient Israel, shade was survival. God is that shade. He stands between you and whatever threatens to burn you up.

The psalm closes with a promise that covers everything: "The LORD will keep you from all harm—he will watch over your life; the LORD will watch over your coming and going both now and forevermore."

Coming and going. Leaving home and arriving at the temple. Setting out and returning. Every step of the journey, in both directions, under God's watchful eye. The word "watch" appears six times in this short psalm. The repetition is the point. God is paying attention. You are not walking unnoticed.

PSALM 133: HOW GOOD AND PLEASANT

Psalm 133 is the shortest of the three, and the simplest. It makes one observation and drives it home with two vivid images. "How good and pleasant it is when God's people live together in unity!"

That's it. That's the thesis. Unity among God's people is good and pleasant. And if you've ever been part of a group that genuinely got along, that worked together and cared for each other, you know exactly what the psalmist is talking about. There's something almost magical about it. Things that would be exhausting alone become energizing together. Burdens that would crush one person get carried easily by many.

The psalmist illustrates unity with two images. The first is oil poured on the head of Aaron, the high priest, so abundant that it runs down his beard and onto his robes. In the ancient world, oil was used to anoint people for sacred service. It represented God's Spirit and blessing. The image here is of that blessing being so overflowing that it covers everything. Unity among God's people is like being drenched in God's blessing.

The second image is dew falling from Mount Hermon, the snowcapped peak in the far north of Israel, down onto Mount Zion in Jerusalem. Hermon was lush and wet. Zion was dry and dusty. Imagine the refreshment of Hermon's moisture reaching Zion. That's what unity does. It brings life to places that were parched.

The psalm ends with a simple statement: "For there the LORD bestows his blessing, even life forevermore." Where God's people are unified, God shows up with his blessing. Unity isn't just nice. It's the place where God does his work.

WHAT THIS MEANS FOR US

First, the journey matters as much as the destination. The Songs of Ascent weren't just about arriving at Jerusalem. They were about being transformed on the way. The Valley of Weeping became a place of springs. The travelers grew stronger as they walked. God doesn't just meet you when you arrive. He meets you on the road.

Second, faith was never meant to be a solo act. The pilgrims didn't walk alone. They traveled in groups, sang together, worshiped together, and carried each other through the hard stretches. If your faith feels lonely, something is missing. God designed worship to be communal. You need the people beside you, and they need you.

Third, God is watching every step. Psalm 121 says it six times because once isn't enough. You are not walking unnoticed. God sees your coming and going, your setting out and your arriving, your good days and your terrible ones. He doesn't sleep. He doesn't look away. He is shade when it's hot and a guard when it's dark.

Fourth, unity is where blessing lives. Psalm 133 doesn't just say unity is pleasant. It says that's where God bestows his blessing. When God's people are divided, fractured, and fighting each other, the blessing dries up. When they come together, when they choose each other despite differences, blessing flows like oil and falls like dew. If you want to be where God is working, find the people who are walking together.

TALKING POINTS

1. **Psalm 84 says the pilgrims turned the Valley of Weeping into a place of springs.** How can difficult seasons in life become something life-giving? Have you ever gone through something hard that turned into something good because of who was with you?

2. **Psalm 121 repeats the idea of God "watching over" you six times.** Why do you think the psalmist said it so many times? What does it feel like to know that God never looks away from you?

3. **The Songs of Ascent were designed to be sung in community on the road to worship.** How is your experience of worship different when you're with other people compared to when you're alone? Why do you think God designed faith to be communal?

4. **Psalm 133 says unity among God's people is like oil flowing down and dew falling on dry ground.** What makes unity so refreshing? Why is it so hard to achieve?

5. **The pilgrims traveled to Jerusalem three times a year, often on dangerous roads.** What does their commitment tell you about how they valued being in God's presence? What "roads" do you have to travel to be present with God's people?

The pilgrim psalms are songs for people who are going somewhere together. They remind us that faith has always been a journey, not just a destination, and the people walking beside you aren't an accident. They're part of the plan.

But there's one more group of psalms we haven't explored yet, the ones that look backward instead of forward. They retell the story of what God has done, not to live in the past, but to make sure the future doesn't forget.

Turn the page.

12

WHEN YOU'RE REMEMBERING

Near the end of James Fenimore Cooper's *The Last of the Mohicans*, a father stands over the body of his son. Chingachgook, the great Mohican chief, is now the last of his people. His son Uncas is dead. The line that stretched back generations, carrying the language, the customs, the memory of an entire nation, now runs through one man alone. If he forgets, everything is lost.

The weight of that moment is almost unbearable. Not just the grief of losing a son, but the terror of losing a story. When the last person who remembers is gone, the story dies with them. Everything a people believed, everything they endured and celebrated and passed down around fires for centuries, disappears as if it never happened.

The writers of the Psalms understood that terror. They knew that the most dangerous thing that could happen to Israel wasn't military defeat or famine or exile. It was forgetting. Forgetting what God had done. Forgetting who they were because of what he'd done. And so they wrote psalms whose entire purpose was to retell the story, to say it again and again until it was branded into the next generation's memory so deeply that nothing could burn it out.

THE PSALMS THAT LOOK BACK

Remembrance psalms are exactly what they sound like. They retell the history of Israel, from Abraham to the conquest, from the exodus to the exile, walking through the major events of God's relationship with his people. They're not history lessons for the sake of information. They're acts of worship. The psalmists retold the past because they believed the past revealed who God is, and knowing who God is changes everything about how you live today.

Two remembrance psalms in particular stand out, and they make for a fascinating comparison. Psalm 78 and Psalm 105 cover much of the same history. They walk through the same events, the same plagues, the same wilderness, the same gift of the land. But they tell the story for completely different reasons. One is a warning. The other is a celebration.

Together, they show that remembering isn't just one thing. How you tell the story matters as much as the story itself.

PSALM 78: SO THEY WON'T REPEAT IT

Psalm 78 is one of the longest psalms in the book, and it opens not with praise but with a classroom. The psalmist positions himself as a teacher passing down essential knowledge:

"My people, hear my teaching; listen to the words of my mouth. I will open my mouth with a parable; I will utter hidden things, things from of old, things we have heard and known, things our ancestors have told us. We will not hide them from their descendants; we will tell the next generation the praiseworthy deeds of the LORD, his power, and the wonders he has done."

The urgency is unmistakable. This is not optional storytelling. This is survival. The psalmist is terrified that if the next generation doesn't hear what God did, they'll make the same catastrophic mistakes their ancestors made.

And then the psalm proves his point by telling the whole ugly story. God performed miracles in Egypt, plagues that brought the most powerful empire on earth to its knees. He split the sea and led his people through it on dry ground. He fed them manna from heaven and brought water from rocks in the desert.

And they forgot. Over and over, they forgot.

"In spite of all this, they kept on sinning; in spite of his wonders, they did not believe." They tested God in the wilderness. They complained about the food. They built an idol while Moses was on the mountain receiving God's law. They grumbled when things got hard and turned to other gods when things got easy.

The cycle is devastating. God rescued them. They forgot. They sinned. God punished them. They cried out. God rescued them again. They forgot again. It kept going, generation after generation, like a wheel that wouldn't stop turning.

The psalm's conclusion explains why this history matters for the present. God eventually rejected the northern kingdom of Israel because of their persistent rebellion and chose Judah instead, establishing David as king and Zion as his holy mountain. The whole point is: don't be like your ancestors. They had every reason to trust God and they didn't. Learn from their failure.

Psalm 78 tells the story of what God's people did wrong so the next generation won't do it again.

PSALM 105: SO THEY'LL NEVER FORGET IT

Psalm 105 covers much of the same ground but sounds completely different. Where Psalm 78 opens with a warning, Psalm 105 opens with a party: "Give thanks to the LORD, call on his name; make known among the nations what he has done. Sing to him, sing praise to him; tell of all his wonderful acts."

Same history. Completely different tone. Psalm 105 isn't interested in Israel's failures. It's interested in God's faithfulness.

The psalm begins with Abraham and the covenant God made with him, the promise that his descendants would become a great nation and inherit the land of Canaan. Then it traces how God kept that promise through every obstacle.

The patriarchs were few in number, wandering through a land that wasn't theirs, vulnerable to every threat. But God protected them. He rebuked kings who threatened them. He watched over them even when they didn't know it.

Then came Joseph. Sold into slavery by his own brothers, thrown into prison on false charges, forgotten by the people he helped. But God was working through every setback. Joseph rose to power in Egypt and saved his entire family from starvation. What looked like the worst thing that could happen turned out to be exactly how God kept his promise alive.

Then came Moses and Aaron. The plagues. The exodus. God splitting the sea, leading his people through the wilderness with a pillar of cloud and fire, feeding them bread from the sky and water from stone. The psalm races through these events with breathless energy, one act of faithfulness stacked on top of another.

And here's what Psalm 105 conspicuously leaves out: the people's rebellion. The grumbling, the golden calf, the constant complaining, none of it appears. Not because it didn't happen, but because this psalm has a different purpose. It's not trying to warn. It's trying to praise. It wants the listener to see the unbroken chain of God's faithfulness from Abraham to the promised land and stand in awe of a God who keeps his word across centuries.

The psalm ends with the conquest: "He gave them the lands of the nations, and they fell heir to what others had toiled for, that they might keep his precepts and observe his laws."

God promised Abraham a nation and a land. It took five hundred years. But he did it.

TWO WAYS TO REMEMBER

These two psalms sit side by side in the Bible like two photographs of the same event taken from different angles.

Psalm 78 looks at the history and asks: What did we do wrong? Its purpose is moral instruction. It wants the next generation to learn from the past so they don't repeat it. The tone is urgent, almost desperate. *Please don't make the same mistakes.*

Psalm 105 looks at the same history and asks: What did God do right? Its purpose is worship. It wants the next generation to see God's faithfulness across centuries and trust him with their own future. The tone is celebratory, almost giddy. *Look at everything he did.*

Both approaches are necessary. If you only tell the warning story, faith becomes fear. If you only tell the celebration story, faith becomes naïve. But together, they give you the full picture: God is unshakably faithful, and we are stubbornly prone to forget that. Remembering both truths keeps you grateful and humble at the same time.

WHAT THIS MEANS FOR US

First, forgetting is the most dangerous thing you can do. The psalmists weren't afraid of armies. They were afraid of amnesia. When God's people forget what he's done, they drift toward the same sins their ancestors committed. Remembering is an act of self-defense against spiritual ruin.

Second, you are responsible to pass the story on. Psalm 78 says explicitly that the purpose of retelling is "so the next generation would know." Your faith isn't just for you. Somewhere behind you is a younger person who needs to hear what God has done. If you stay silent, the chain breaks.

Third, the same history can teach different lessons depending on how you tell it. Sometimes you need to hear "don't make the same mistake." Sometimes you need to hear "look how faithful God has been." Wisdom is knowing which version you need today.

Fourth, God's faithfulness outlasts everything. Psalm 105 spans five hundred years of history and the conclusion is simple: God kept his promise. He kept it through famine, slavery, exile, wandering, and war. If you're wondering whether God will come through for you, look back. The track record is long, and it's flawless.

TALKING POINTS

1. **Psalm 78 says the biggest danger for God's people is forgetting what he's done.** Why do you think forgetting is so easy? What are some ways you can build remembering into your daily life?

2. **Psalm 105 tells the story of Israel without mentioning any of the people's failures.** Why do you think the psalmist made that choice? Is it dishonest to leave out the bad parts, or is there a good reason for it?

3. **The two psalms cover the same events but with completely different purposes, one as a warning and one as praise.** Which approach do you connect with more right now? Why?

4. **Psalm 78 was written specifically "so the next generation would know."** Who in your life has passed down stories of faith to you? Is there someone younger who might need to hear your story?

5. **Psalm 105 traces God's faithfulness across five hundred years.** What are some things God has done in your life, or in the life of your family or church, that you never want to forget?

The remembrance psalms are the Bible's way of saying: *Don't you dare forget this.* The story of what God has done is too important to let it fade. It needs to be told, retold, and told again, in warning and in praise, until the next generation knows it as well as you do.

We've walked through every kind of psalm in the book. Praise, lament, thanksgiving, trust, confession, anger, wisdom, kingship, pilgrimage, and remembrance. But there's one more thing to say. One final word about what all of this means and what to do when you open the Psalms for yourself.

Turn the page.

13

WHEN YOU NEED WORDS AND DON'T HAVE ANY

Have you ever needed to say something to God and had absolutely no idea how to start? Maybe something terrible happened and you sat on the edge of your bed staring at the wall, wanting to pray but not knowing what to say. Maybe something wonderful happened, and "thank you" felt too small, but you couldn't think of anything bigger. Maybe you just felt far from God, like he was on the other side of a thick door, and you didn't know the right knock.

It's one of the strangest experiences of faith: believing that an infinite God hears you and still not knowing what to say to him. Your feelings are too big, or too tangled, or too raw. You open your mouth and nothing comes out. Or worse, the only words that come feel shallow, like sending a smiley-face emoji when what you really need to say would take a hundred pages.

The Psalms were written for that moment.

A PRAYER BOOK FOR EVERY SEASON

We've spent several chapters walking through the kinds of songs that fill this book. Praise psalms for the moments when you can't stop marveling at who God is. Laments for the moments when you can barely hold on. Thanksgiving psalms for the days after God answers. Trust psalms for the dark nights when all you have is a grip on his character. Penitential psalms for the devastating honesty of confession. Imprecatory psalms for the rage you don't know what to do with. Wisdom psalms for the slow, hard work of figuring out how to live. Royal psalms for the king who was coming. Pilgrim psalms for the journey you take with others. Remembrance psalms for the story you must never let die.

One hundred and fifty songs. Every emotion. Every season. Every kind of day a human being can have.

And here's the thing most people miss: the Psalms weren't just written to be studied. They were written to be prayed. They're not a textbook about prayer. They *are* prayer. Every psalm is an invitation to open your mouth and make someone else's words your own.

BORROWING SOMEONE ELSE'S WORDS

This might feel strange at first. Praying someone else's words can seem less personal than coming up with your own. But think about it. When you sing a hymn at church, you're singing words someone else wrote. When you pray the Lord's Prayer, you're praying words Jesus gave his disciples. You're not being fake. You're being formed. Someone who knew how to say it better than you handed you the words, and as you say them, they become yours.

The Psalms work the same way. When you're devastated and can't articulate why, Psalm 13 gives you the words: "How long, LORD? Will you forget me forever?" When you're overwhelmed by the beauty of a night sky, Psalm 19 hands you: "The heavens declare the glory of God." When you're terrified and need to remind yourself what's true, Psalm 46 is right there: "God is our refuge and strength, an ever-present help in trouble." When guilt is eating you alive, Psalm 51 says what you can't: "Create in me a pure heart, O God."

You don't have to feel everything perfectly before you pray a psalm. Sometimes you pray the words first and the feelings catch up later. Sometimes you start reading Psalm 42 because you know you're supposed to, and halfway through you realize the psalmist is describing exactly what's happening inside you. The words find you. They name what you couldn't name. And suddenly you're not praying someone else's prayer anymore. It's yours.

People have been doing this for three thousand years. David did it. The sons of Korah did it. Jewish families did it around their dinner tables. Early Christians did it in their house churches. Monks in medieval monasteries chanted the entire book of Psalms every week. Reformers like Martin Luther called the Psalms "a little Bible" and built their prayer lives around them. Prisoners, soldiers, grieving parents, joyful newlyweds, and scared children have all opened this book and found the words they needed waiting for them.

You can too.

THE BOOK THAT BENDS TOWARD PRAISE

One more thing about the Psalms that's easy to miss if you only read individual songs: the whole book tells a story.

We talked about this in the first chapter, but it's worth saying again now that you've walked through every type of psalm. The first half of the book is heavy with laments. Cries of pain, confusion, and abandonment dominate the early psalms. If you started reading at Psalm 1 and kept going, you'd spend a lot of time in the dark.

But as you move deeper into the collection, something shifts. Praise starts showing up more frequently. Trust pushes through the grief. Thanksgiving answers the laments. By the time you reach the final five psalms, lament has disappeared entirely. Psalms 146–150 are nothing but praise, and Psalm 150 is the most explosive worship song in the Bible, every instrument playing, every breath praising, every living thing joining the chorus.

The book starts in the valley and ends on the mountaintop. It starts with "How long?" and ends with "Praise the Lord!" The pain was real. The darkness was real. But it wasn't the last word. Praise was.

That's not wishful thinking. It's the shape of reality as the Bible understands it. Suffering is temporary. God's love is permanent. Weeping lasts for a night, but joy comes in the morning. The whole book of Psalms bends toward praise because the whole story of God bends toward restoration. One day, every tear will be wiped away, every wrong will be made right, and every voice will join the final psalm.

We're not there yet. You might be reading this in the middle of your own lament season. But the Psalms promise that the music will change. Hold on long enough, and the song becomes praise.

WHERE JESUS MEETS YOU

Throughout this book, we've watched for Jesus in the Psalms. He's everywhere.

He's the Good Shepherd of Psalm 23, the one who walks through the valley with you. He's the King of Psalm 2, installed on God's holy mountain with the nations as his inheritance. He's the suffering servant of Psalm 22, crying "My God, my God, why have you forsaken me?" from the cross. He's the priest forever of Psalm 110, seated at God's right hand. He's the one Psalm 72 was waiting for, the king so just and compassionate that no human ruler could fill the role. He's the living water that Psalm 42's thirsty deer was panting for.

When Jesus was dying, he reached for the Psalms. When the early church wanted to explain who he was, they quoted the Psalms more than almost any other book. When the New Testament writers looked back at Jesus' life, they saw psalm after psalm lighting up like someone had finally turned on the lights in a room that had been furnished for centuries but never fully seen.

The Psalms were waiting for him. And now that he's come, every psalm you read has a deeper layer. The shepherd has a name. The king has a face. The rescue has been accomplished. The praise that ends the book has a reason that the original psalmists could only dream about.

When you pray the Psalms, you're praying words that Jesus himself prayed. You're joining a conversation that stretches from David's harp to the throne room of heaven. You're adding your voice to a chorus that has never stopped singing.

YOUR TURN

So here you are. You've made it through the whole book. You know what the Psalms are, who wrote them, how they're organized, and what kinds of songs they contain. You know about parallelism and metaphor and the difference between praise and thanksgiving. You know about laments and trust psalms and the terrifying honesty of the imprecatory prayers. You know the Psalms point to Jesus and that the whole collection bends from pain toward praise.

Now what?

Open the book. Not this book. *The* book. Open your Bible to the Psalms and start reading. You don't have to start at Psalm 1, though you can. Pick the psalm that matches where you are today. If you're amazed, read Psalm 19. If you're hurting, read Psalm 13. If you're scared, read Psalm 23. If you're grateful, read Psalm 30. If you're angry, read Psalm 137. If you need to confess, read Psalm 51. If you need to remember what God has done, read Psalm 105. If you just want to worship, read Psalm 150.

Read it once for the feel. Read it again for the details. Watch how the second line sharpens the first. Look for the images. Put yourself inside the poem. And then do something the psalmists have been inviting people to do for three thousand years.

Pray it.

Say the words out loud. Make them yours. Let them name the thing inside you that you couldn't name on your own. You don't need perfect faith or a clean record or a theology degree. You just need honesty and an open Bible.

The Psalms have been waiting a very long time for you to walk in.

The door is open.

www.ingramcontent.com/pod-product-compliance
Lightning Source LLC
Chambersburg PA
CBHW051812050726
47598CB00006B/2523